At the Edge
of Our Longing

FRESH WISDOM FOR TOMORROW

JIM CONLON

At the Edge of Our Longing
By Jim Conlon

©2023 Jim Conlon

ISBN: 979-8-9864100-6-7

My Springbank Prayer

Through vision, passion, dream, and prayer, may this sacred place be where I grow my soul and discover my true self through beauty, healing, and cosmic creativity.

Contents

i

Foreword

I am fascinated by the title of this book. It evokes several connections with what modern scientists call "the edge of chaos," which does not describe the onset of chaos but its aftereffects. Chaos theory describes a state of internal dislocation, because the old certainties don't make sense anymore. The order begins to disintegrate, disorder ensues, and the system veers toward a freshly discovered sense of coherence.

This is the edge of chaos. The old will never be the same again, but the new is still unfolding, sometimes confusing, chaotic, stretching, even exciting. It is not neat and precise like the old order, but intuition tells us that it is a great deal more real, and this is what compels credibility.

Jim Conlon brings a creative and intuitive mind to this "edge of our longing," but he goes beyond the *longing* into the realm of *belonging*. And the belonging is no longer just personal, interpersonal, or social. It is planetary, global, and cosmic. This is Conlon's revolutionary insight. Moving through the four spheres of soul, life, Earth, and the divine, the psychologist within me hears resonances of stages of developmental growth. The difference, of course, is that these are planetary/cosmic stages and not merely personal ones.

This is precisely what the edge of chaos is about. The previous, familiar world of conventional wisdom no longer holds. The certainties crumble, the clarity fades, the boundaries are stretched, often beyond recognition. We are into new territory: disturbing, dangerous, challenging, but for growing numbers among us, exciting and promising. Assuredly, we have been there before, and nobody knows the territory better than the mystics, both ancient and recent. Jim Conlon graciously acknowledges their enduring contribution.

But even for the mystics, there is a radical newness. We encounter a new evolutionary movement that is beginning to dawn upon our world. None of us has been there before. We need fresh wisdom for our time and for our journey. You would be advised to take along a copy of *At the Edge of Our Longing*. You'll find it a useful resource; solace for the turbulent times; guidance at the crossroads; and above all, reassurance for the different future that embraces our world in these opening decades of the twenty-first century.

Diarmuid O'Murchu
June 2004

At the Edge
of Our Longing

Prologue

We live in a world that seems bent on its own destruction, that has abandoned its wisdom sources and the healing power of intimacy and contemplation in relationship to soul, life, Earth, and the divine.

It is a world marked by a new age of anxiety whose defining moments are the erosion of democracy, a global pandemic, and looming climate disasters, a world where reverence for the child as the icon of hope has been squandered through acts of violence and abuse.

A world where the vision of a better tomorrow has collapsed in daily reports of global conflict, ecological degradation manifest in poisoned water, toxic air and land, the new viral variants.

A world where participation in the great work, humanity's historical mission, has been reduced to monitoring economic indicators and the spread of hate speech online.

In the words of Rainer Maria Rilke, I discovered a title for these pages and a spiritual strategy for responding to the dislocation that many of us experience today. I suggest that it is by reflecting on and responding to our experience of longing that we will develop a spirituality for living in and transforming today's world. Longing is a theme that permeates our cultural soul. We are being invited to remain balanced in our quest for intimacy and contemplation.

Through intimacy, we commune deeply. Relationships become the monasteries where we deepen our discovery of meaning and purpose. Through intimacy, we fall in love with soul, life, Earth, and the divine and embrace fully the joys and sorrows, beauty and pain, of existence. Our experience of intimacy will be complemented by our experience of contemplation, liberation, and creation.

In contemplation, we embrace silence and stillness, we quiet the mind and penetrate the fault lines of the psyche. Through intimacy, we gain fresh energy and move forward to heal a broken world.

When our experience of intimacy, contemplation, liberation, and creation is understood within the context of the universe, we are transported from any tendency toward self-centeredness and enter into a world that is vast and cosmic. This journey of solitude and communion will move us forward into new frontiers of sacredness and depth.

As we embrace the balanced experience of intimacy and contemplation within the context of the universe, we cross the threshold into a mystical cosmology of sacredness and depth. We find an engaged spirituality whereby we become one with our soul, with life, with creation, and with the divine. When intimacy and contemplation are viewed from a perspective that integrates quantum physics, evolutionary science, psychology, theology, and cultural analysis, it culminates in an approach I call *engaged cosmology*.

It is my hope that the mystical and engaged cosmology discovered from experiencing the longing of soul, life, Earth, and divine can become a spiritual resource through which we view our life in the larger cosmic context and feel a healthy sense of responsibility for the planet.

As we listen and, in the words of Thomas Merton, "get a glimpse of the cosmic dance," we realize that our longing, as John O'Donohue said, "echoes the divine longing."

Nourished by the realization that we are engaged in a spiritual journey named by the poets, lived by the prophets, and revealed by the universe, we move forward to heal and transform the world.

In our longing for sacredness and depth, we explore and experience:

- Soul, in those contemplative moments that touch the heart and prompt us to change and grow
- Life, through opportunities to transcend anxiety and become liberated from everyday confusions, to embrace relationship and wisdom
- Earth, in communion with creation as the source and sign of ecological harmony, balance, and peace
- Divine, as the vulnerable and receptive one, calling us into relationship and into the experience of contemplation, liberation, and creation, inviting us to belong and instilling in us the courage to confront the challenge of the day

At the Edge of Our Longing is an invitation to embark on a common journey and to melt into our individual consciousness a cosmic awareness. May we draw courage from each other and enchantment from creation as we open ourselves to the surging miracle of life.

The Genesis

When I first conceived of this book twenty years ago, I envisioned what I thought at the time would be an ideal sabbatical for myself. I imagined taking a journey to visit the people and locations where the most significant and prophetic spiritual work was being done. On this journey, I would explore three theological approaches and create a synthesis of them in the context of the new universe story. The first three chapters of this book would represent these three approaches, and the fourth chapter would represent their synthesis.

My imagined sabbatical began at Gethsemane Abbey, near Bardstown, Kentucky, where I wanted to spend time with the work of Thomas Merton. I was there in 1965, when Merton was alive. During the feast of Corpus Christi, the monastic cloister was carpeted with petals as we slowly proceeded, with the monstrance containing the host in gratitude for the gift of the Eucharist. Intuitively, I knew the contemplative life at Gethsemane provided an opportunity to pay attention to the presence of God and explore the deeper recesses of my soul, and the interdependence of all things, within the Catholic tradition in which I was raised.

I also knew, as the Buddhists say, that "action without prayer is a fragile thing." I knew that the contemplative journey is necessary if we as a people are going to be able to engage in the great issues of our time (race, gender, class, health, war and peace, ecological devastation) and confront the dark night of our cultural soul that permeates this moment. Merton wrote in his final book that the "inarticulate longing for Him in the night of suffering will be your most eloquent prayer." With these words, he named the first step on the journey: *the longing of soul.*

The second step on my imagined sabbatical was to go to Peru to visit the Institute of Bartholome de Las Casas and Gustavo Gutiérrez, the recognized father of liberation theology. In Latin America and among oppressed peoples around the world, liberation theology has stirred a fresh commitment to freedom, dignity, destiny, and fulfillment. Gutiérrez described the liberation process as the commitment to "think through our faith, to strengthen our love, and to give reason for our hope." He reminded us that the experience of oppression is incompatible with the Christian tradition, and that faith and life are inseparable. He stated that liberation involves freedom from a death that is both physical and spiritual. It demands access to food, housing, health care, education, workers' rights, employment, and self-expression in both politics and religion.

Liberation theology is guided by the principle of a preferential option for the poor. With this in mind, we acknowledge the presence of divinity among those lowest on the social ladder, the most abused of society. We also realize that the fullest experience of liberation has three important dimensions: freedom from internalized oppression (intrapsychic), freedom in relationship to others and the structures of society, and freedom in our relationship with the divine. In these ways, liberation theology names the second step on the journey: *the longing of life.*

The third step on my sabbatical journey took me back to the Riverdale Center for Religious Research for conversations with Thomas Berry and to the Learning Center at Genesis Farm in New Jersey, where Miriam MacGillis and her colleagues invite us to explore the new cosmology and its implications for our lives. This step also included conversations with Thomas Berry,

Rosemary Radford, Brian Thomas Swimme, and others, as well as the opportunity to read and reread their work.

This third step in the journey is named *the longing of Earth*. As we view the world through the lens of creation theology, our perception of the world is transformed. We go beyond soul and life to include our relationship with the natural world. We enter the world of creation theology as the sun greets us each morning, as the kitten warms itself by the window seat, as the clouds choreograph the sky, and as dusk guides us onto the threshold of night. We realize anew that a fully healed, liberated person cannot exist without a healed and liberated Earth. We experience each expression of creation as sacred, and we are bathed in the wonder and awe of creation. The words of Hildegard of Bingen take on new meaning: "Every creature is illuminated by the brightness." With this in mind, we celebrate the whole world as sacrament, with humans as interdependent members of the Earth community collaborating fully in its future and well-being.

Upon reflection, it is apparent that the genesis of a mystical and engaged cosmology is aligned with the principles of the cosmos. In this way, contemplation is related to interiority (sentience and spontaneity), liberation to differentiation (unending variety), and creation to communion (everything is related). Each is interconnected within the context of the universe itself.

The fourth step, *the longing of the divine*, is the culminating section of these pages. Here, we re-vision each of the previous steps (soul/contemplation, life/liberation, and Earth/creation) from a new cosmological perspective. In the longing of soul, we understand the psyche (soul) to be coextensive with the universe. In the longing of life, we extend our view of liberation to embrace the entire Earth community, including every species. In the longing of Earth, we celebrate a sacramental consciousness that sees each moment as revelatory. We gain access to fresh psychic energy and a new awareness to move forward to create and transform the world.

The longing of the divine is a synthesis of contemplative liberation and creation theology within the context of the universe itself. We move forward to participate in an engaged cosmology and create a strategy for a just and peaceful world: a world of geo-justice, where the dynamics of the universe are a template for harmony, balance, and peace; a world of engagement, where we are empowered by the universe to fashion a new creation and heal the face of Earth.

My Second Exodus

As I reflected more, I realized we have among us people whose work continues to embody the hoped-for results of my imagined sabbatical. The many resources and desires I wanted to pursue in far-off places are right here with us, and their work is available and present. And so, without getting on an airplane or train or boat, I wrote the first edition of *At the Edge of Our Longing*, which was published by Novalis in 2004.

In its essence, *At the Edge of Our Longing* offers a dynamic integration of the longing of soul, life, Earth, and the divine, culminating in a spectrum theology that is expressed through an engaged cosmology.

Now, two decades later, I find this message to be as relevant and needed—if not more so—in the world today, so I have refreshed my initial contemplations and offer them to you in this second edition.

I continue to draw sustenance from the work of Thomas Berry, who proposed that, through our experience of Earth, we can awaken to a fresh dimension of soul, to a sacred interiority where dreams and aspirations are infused with holy mystery. May his vision evoke in each of us a poetic response that is true and authentic.

Thomas Merton urged us to awaken the dormant inner depths of the spirit through seeds of contemplation, while Gustavo Gutiérrez heard the call of the oppressed and formulated what became known as liberation theology.

Drawing on their vast combined wisdom, I believe we can learn to engage in the transformation of the world through a dynamic synthesis that I propose to call an expression of *spectrum theology*, a term I first heard used by a Sister of Mercy from New Zealand, Anne Campbell.

Part 1
Longing of Soul

Canticle to Soul

Let us...

Give voice to our unspoken hunger,
to our quest for sacredness and depth,
Keep on believing in the fruitfulness of our efforts,
join with those who are willing
to risk their lives and lifestyles,
that others may flourish and live.
Become sensitive to the poverty of the planet
and listen to people in pain.
Nurture new expressions of compassion
and cocreate structures of peace.
Become fully present to those we love,
nurture a new spirituality
to energize a world
of harmony, balance, and peace.
Celebrate Earth as a living community
and our common home.
Practice nonviolence and celebrate each moment
as an epiphany of kindness, beauty, listening, and love.
Remember our story and
let go of anything that stands in the way
of living fully, with a listening heart.
Search for the subtle presence of the divine,
especially in the cry of the poor,
who allow the divine to shine through.
Search for sacredness and depth,
where the unspoken hunger reveals
the language of connectedness, cosmology, and soul.

And we will discover who we really are.

Moments of Sacredness and Depth

Soul happens in relationship, in moments of intimacy and of solitude. As we remember these experiences, they touch our heart, and our spirit soars. We imagine healing all separateness. We are embraced in the genuine depths of compassion, home, silence, friendship, and inclusion. Soul becomes a compass of hope.

The longing of soul can be best understood through the lens of contemplative theology. Here, we focus our conscious attention on the presence of the divine in all things. As we respond to the longing of the soul, we integrate our experience through a deeper awareness of the interior life and the mystery of existence.

In contemplation, we commune with cosmic forces, with the ultimate mystery. We practice a spirituality born out of the depths of the universe in moments of intimacy and solitude.

Balm for the Soul

Deep within the restless world,
resides a profound pursuit,
an uncommon quest
for intimacy and rest,
a longing for peace,
relief for the journey,
a search for oneness,
a loving embrace
that heals the heart,
a balm for the soul,
that longs to just be,
a sabbath for the soul.

A Sabbath for the Soul

Our souls are shaped by the stories we hear and by the stories we tell ourselves. These narratives give shape to who we are in our own eyes. They also name the sequence of events that tell others about us, and identify who we are to the world.

A primary threshold to freedom is telling our story differently. Our story can include our accomplishments and help us emerge from the closet of self-deprecation. It can transform a self-taught litany of failure into a banquet of blessings. Our story can announce our presence as an unexpected moment when grace entered our lives. It can provide a sabbath for the soul in the midst of turbulence.

These moments of sabbath and rest happen when the longing of the soul is quenched and we are one with our heart's pursuit.

These mystical moments heal the heart and envelop us in a mystery that alters and illuminates our lives.

For you, these moments may bring to mind the beauty of the stars, the trajectory of a swallow in flight, the arching leap of a pickerel from silken waters as the sun recedes in the West.

Or it may be a moment in the backyard with your baseball coach, as you listened eagerly to his reflections on the game of life.

Or perhaps moments of portent and prophecy while following in the footsteps of Dr. Martin Luther King, Jr., on Woodward Avenue in Detroit, Michigan, when your heart opened and imagination soared to embrace the social gospel as a vehicle to alter and illuminate our lives.

After years of study and reflection, there may be a moment in which mystical and engaged cosmology becomes more than words. Suddenly, as if for the first time, we become one with the star, the sunset, the bird, the fish, the mentor. We see in each, the God who came down from heaven, and in each, we experience a sabbath for the soul.

The Closing of the Prison Door

The capacity to listen and respond with an open heart reveals much about ourselves and our capacity for generosity and compassion.

This incident, which was told to me by an Irish official, occurred when the inmates of Mount Joy Women's Prison in Dublin, Ireland, were being transferred to a new facility. On Christmas Eve, during the closing of the prison, an older woman prisoner stepped forward and declared to the man in charge, "I want to close the door for the last time!"

When he asked why, she declared, "I have the right. My grandmother was here, my mother was here, my sisters were here, my baby sister was born here, and I'm here!"

Following her plea, she was selected to close the door for the last time.

At the new prison after the liturgy on Christmas Day, she clung to a photo of her closing the door and walked around showing it to everyone present. It was a sad yet powerful moment. On a day for remembering the birth of the liberating Christ, she was proud of being selected to close the door to the prison that had housed the women of her family over so many years.

This story reminds us of our need to be chosen, to be recognized, to have our value acknowledged. This need for respect sometimes shows up in unpredictable ways. This prisoner challenges us to cultivate a willingness to listen with our hearts, to accept the humanity of the other—their value, experience, wisdom, pain, and unrealized potential. It inspires us to discover and experience satisfaction by bringing hope, contentment, and appreciation of the other.

Prisoners are often looked upon as dangerous and damaged people without status, esteem, or respectability. It is important to listen to them, to realize that each of us in our way is "doing time." Each of us is imprisoned in the cellblock of internalized oppression, the iron cage of the system that lives within.

Grace Happens

Grace happens when we explore the deep inner currents of belonging and realize the profound connection between our aspirations for life and the concrete requirements for living.

Grace happens in possible and sometimes impossible ways.

Grace happens when our mood shifts and we discover new people and projects in seemingly mysterious ways.

Grace happens when we discover anew that life has its own trajectory and that we know deeply that we live in a universe where we are not in charge.

Grace happens when we discover that life requires effort in what often feels like effortless ways.

Grace happens when we work hard, stay focused, yet realize the outcomes are far beyond our awareness, energies, or control.

Grace happens as a gift, a manifestation of an unfolding universe whose ultimate trajectory is always toward the good.

Grace happens when life becomes embedded in mystery and surprise.

Grace happens when we awaken to many questions and are willing to remain uncertain yet in pursuit of the quest.

Grace happens when in our soul-searching, we find a way to heal the wounds of childhood.

Grace happens when science speaks to us and reveals its many patterns on our path.

Grace happens when in the midst of our search, we discover that place of hope where our secret longings lie.

Grace happens when in our restlessness, we discover colleagues in pursuit of justice who also long for a life of harmony, balance, and peace.

Grace happens when we discover at the threshold of unexplored frontiers a quantum realm wherein reside the secrets of what it means to be alive.

Grace happens when we embark anew on a journey to celebrate fresh expressions of wisdom, to see each expression of creation as a unique manifestation of sacredness and new life.

Dispelling the Darkness

The winter solstice has a profound impact on our souls. On the shortest day of the year, darkness permeates Earth. It is a time when we pause to consider how events of our time have spread fear and terror across our darkened land.

I think of an elderly woman sitting alone in a dark apartment in Kyiv, listening for the next air raid siren. Meanwhile a little boy in Nashville pleads with his parents to let him stay home from school because he's afraid a shooter will come to his classroom. And a young woman tells her new husband she doesn't want children because their lives would be filled with suffering from climate disaster.

The winter solstice is also the time when the sun begins to return to Earth, a powerful symbol reminding us of the Son of God coming to Earth on that first Christmas.

Reflections at the Edge of Soul

The spiritual journey contains a variety of ingredients: courage, openness, compassion, integral consciousness, and love. These are the expression of a generous and abundant universe.

Through mystical engagement, we contemplate the depths of the psyche and receive images, symbols, and archetypes from the wellspring of our soul.

As we bring to conscious expression what lies in the recesses of our psyches, we fashion a holistic spirituality that is aligned to the cosmos, resides within the soul, and culminates in a compassionate commitment to the prophetic struggle.

At the heart of our spiritual journey resides the longing to belong and to live a meaningful and joyful life. Simultaneously, there springs up within the soul of our culture a profound aspiration to transcend limitations and embrace the mystery that is constantly in our midst. When we encounter the fault line between mystery and comprehension, many questions emerge. They invite us to reflect more deeply on the relationship between:

- Intimacy and contemplation
- Engagement and detachment
- Feminism and pro-male attitudes
- Poetry and politics
- The great work and right livelihood
- Our personal journey and the new story
- Mystical cosmology and the life of engagement
- Vocation and living meaningfully in a dislocated culture
- Spirituality and religion

Our journey toward a healthy, functional future requires an openness to new states of consciousness, to welcoming the unexpected in our lives, whether insights, actions, or relationships. We are also invited to consider deeply the impact of a living cosmology (a new vision for life) that sees all of creation functioning in an interrelated, mutually enhancing, and interdependent way. This perspective sheds light on our place in the unfolding drama of the universe. It is a worldview that generates gratitude and fresh psychic energy for the challenges that lie ahead.

We can understand this energy as a fire that burns deeply with passion and compassion to heal the wounds of the human and other-than-human world. This energy evokes within us a new mystical cosmology that is the ground for a fluid and fruitful integration of intimacy and contemplation, a crucible for a life charged with beauty, vision, and divine presence. We are enriched when we explore deeply the longing that penetrates our souls, our lives, our planet, and the divine.

It is commonly understood that crises can provide opportunities for change and assist us to move forward in new and unprecedented ways, to see things differently, and subsequently to act differently. As we look back upon the rubble of a post-industrial age, we see what we have done and perhaps ask why we are here and what we are called to do in the face of a dangerous yet hopeful future. The crisis of cultural degeneration invites us to engage in the work of transformation and become people with listening hearts. This work will nurture a renewed sensitivity and our capacity to take up the challenge of healing the tragedy we have caused.

We extend our awareness and compassion beyond the human and generously respond to this moment of grace and opportunity for transformation. With a renewed sense of awe and wonder, we work to transform the dominant cultural paradigm.

Gratitude for a Hungry Heart

I want to encourage you
and give thanks for your hungry heart,
for the longing you feel,
for the beauty you are,
for the soul you hope to become,
for the broken heart that is always open
to the beauty and pain of the world.

Is this not the time to burst into song
for all who dare to listen?
Give holy mystery a voice
as you embrace a silent thanks
and welcome what is still unknown.
As you awaken from a silent slumber,
know that the trees welcome you.

A Deeper Life

We ask, "Where is my place in the universe? What am I here for? And what the indicators will help me understand and feel at peace?" Many of us spend our lives in a state of unclarity. Achieving clarity doesn't involve manipulating the universe to our own ends. It's a process of discovery that continues to unfold.

Mary Oliver's poem "The Journey" explores the dream from a mythological and cosmological perspective. She reminds us that the challenge is to take our life in our own hands. When we do, we have a greater capacity to fulfill our life purpose. She reminds us not to listen to bad advice but to listen to our inner voice for the invitation, the vocation, the calling. A vocation is a calling, a voice from outside that summons us.

When our calling comes, we might be asked to take our life into our own hands just when things seem least clear to us. Pain and loss often open the door to our true self. Ernesto Cardinale, the great Nicaraguan poet, says that when we hear the call, we will be prompted by our discontent. Something in us will tell us that we've been off course. When we become physically ill, we know there's something wrong. The same thing is true of our life's direction: if we're troubled in our hearts, then something is off course.

Often the very significant things that change our life seem insignificant at the moment they happen. When we look back later, we recognize them as turning points. It could have been a phone call, a gesture, an insight, a trip, a moment when we took a new direction, or when we knew what we had to do and began.

The voice of vocation doesn't lead us to exactly where our heroes have been. We're not here to be another Gandhi, or Dr. King, or Teresa of Avila, or Mother Teresa. Though we might be inspired by such people, inspiration is not authentic if it leads only to a rigid imitation. The challenge is not to repeat their lives but to learn how they brought them about, how they changed the culture to make their vision a possibility. That's the imitation that our ancestors are calling us to.

How can we be true to ourselves? Mary Oliver says that we are here "to save the only life you could save." To me, that means being true to our inner wisdom, promptings, and indicators—the moments of synchronicity and the sacred impulses that guide us toward the future. Most of us have tapes inside us—the voices of our parents, of institutions, of authority figures—that have conditioned us to respond in ways that are less than authentic. What is authentic is often what we know for certain without being able to explain why. From that knowing, we stride deeper and deeper into the world. "To save the only life that you could save" is to answer your calling.

Vocation in our world is usually associated with a job. We define ourselves by our functions, our professions. But we are not what we do for a living. One of the ways to ask yourself what you are called to is to see what you are preoccupied with, what you are passionate about, what you are competent in. What are your gifts? What are you committed to? The call to a deeper life is not about the external lifestyle choices you have made. It's not about your religious life or whether you are married or single. It's about the call within the call, about what summons each of us to be our authentic self.

Unfortunately, many of the contexts available for us do not support our inner promptings. We have to change society so we can have a context for our calling. As we change paradigms and cosmologies, we also change the context in which we live our lives. Our lives must be culturally connected to the unfolding of the universe.

Nelson Mandela didn't become bitter during his years of imprisonment. He stayed a prophet in the cell block. We too are in the cell blocks of our own culture. We're all doing time. We're incarcerated in the oppressive structures of our society. We can learn to emancipate ourselves and the oppressive forces around us. This is our task, our call to deeper life.

A Time Alone

A time alone to ponder
purpose, place, and me.
A time alone to ponder
what will be revealed to see.
A time alone to ponder
the book that is my hungry soul.
A time alone to ponder
the beauty of a rose.
A time alone to ponder
my longings at the edge.
A time alone to ponder
the universe and its call.
A time alone to ponder
what it means just to be.
A time alone to ponder
the unspoken sacredness of life.

Growing Our Soul

An integral spirituality identifies and responds to issues that have an impact on the planet and our lives. It evokes imagination and courage. It is written in the narrative of people's lives and inscribed in the story of the universe. It is nurtured by passion, moral outrage, and hope. It is discovered and expressed through trust, listening, and soul work. It finds expression in a newfound freedom for people and the planet.

When I was a young boy growing up in Ontario, Canada, I lived on the baseball diamond. My brother and I often visited the man who was our coach and talked with him about life. One day, I arrived to find his wife, Dorothy, walking around in the backyard, under the apple trees. I asked her what she was doing, and she said, "I'm just out here in the backyard growing my soul."

My question for us is "How do we grow our soul?" What was Dorothy talking about, and what can we learn from her?

There are some spiritual practices I'd like to highlight that contribute to our journey into sacredness and depth, including listening, heeding the prophets, letting go, remembering, exercising compassion, relating to the little ones, making authentic rituals, celebrating creativity, honoring the beauty of creation, and harboring hope and vision.

Listening

Listening is the capacity not just to hear with our ears but to be open to whatever and wherever the universe chooses to communicate with us. It could be from a bird, a breeze, a tree, or in the prophetic voice of a Dr. Martin Luther King, Jr., or a Mahatma Gandhi, or in the canonical texts of our traditions, whether the Hebrew or Christian Bible, the Quran, or the ancestral voices. Such a listening heart also enables us to attend to the promptings of our own souls. Intuition—the capacity to be open to what some call "that still small voice"—is an expression of such listening.

Part of listening is giving recognition to another. Listening is not about giving advice. When someone talks about their life, you don't need to have answers for them. They aren't really looking for that from you. They just want someone to listen. Most of us have our own answers; we long for an opportunity to access the clarity that exists deep within us. That clarity comes through being listened to and being able to listen to ourselves. Recognition provides the attention that makes the listening possible. It's both a great challenge and also a priceless gift just to listen.

One definition for spirituality is the capacity for a listening heart. The listening heart is sensitive and receptive to all of the interactions and relationships we both endure and celebrate. We listen with the ears of the soul. Listening and recognition are profound ways to grow our soul. Brother David Steindl-Rast says that a listening heart involves the experience of faith, hope, and love through existential trust, openness to surprise, and saying yes to belonging.

Heeding the Prophets

Another way to grow our soul is to listen to and to be inspired by the voices of the prophets. Dom Helder Camara, the Bishop of Recife in Brazil, who was one of the great voices of the poor in the church after Vatican II, wrote, "Anytime, day or night, at home or in the street, wherever we are, we live bathed in God." That is the voice of a prophet.

It is important to understand that neither the prophets of the Old Testament, Daniel and Samuel and Isaiah, nor the prophets or our time—such as Dr. King, Gandhi, Dorothy Day, Cesar Chavez, Bede Griffith, Thomas Merton, and perhaps your own ancestors—are asking us to imitate them. They are asking us to be inspired by our own vision, energized by their words so we can find our own way, our own response to this prophetic moment, whether it be in the church, the workplace, the family, or the society that truly needs our help. Rabbi Heschel, the great Jewish mystic, said, "Let there be a grain of prophet" in each human soul. Such a vision calls upon us to be a people of protest and prophecy, to stand on our principles, to speak truth to power, and to dare to tell the truth.

Imagine a volcano like the ones in Hawaii. When it is erupting, everything is fluid and warm and moving. After a while, however, the flow turns to rock; it becomes rigid and stuck. We need theological air hammers to release the molten places underneath the crust of tradition so we can uncover the prophetic voice that is still fluid—the passionate voice of compassion that is reaching out to the little ones.

Today, our prophetic voices need to stand on the side of the planet and the people who cry out for a new world community.

Letting Go

Almost every tradition has a practice of letting go, even if it uses different language to describe it. Buddhism talks about the danger of attachment, which could also be described as clinging. It is our clinging, not the object of our attachment, that is the problem. One of the reasons we have a pathological culture is our collective inability to let go.

Culture is made up of many elements that differ from people to people: different music, different ancestral myths, different creation stories, different art forms, different rituals, different values, different ethics and customs. Our spirituality is intimately connected to all these cultural elements. It's embodied and it's contextualized. If we judge some element of our culture to be pathological, we need to seek a spiritual practice that will allow us to heal the illness we experience. One such practice is the process of letting go.

In the life of the medieval mystic John of the Cross, we find a powerful example of the practice of letting go. He suffered abuse, pain, and incarceration, but he did not hold onto anger, bitterness, or despair. John of the Cross wrote about what he called "the dark night of the soul." Some would describe the dark night as the experience of falling out of a plane and fearing your parachute won't open. We're living today in the dark night of our cultural soul, as well as of our personal experiences. We need to learn to break through our fear, to let go of the unnecessary limitations we place on our envisioning of what life can be.

Two examples of such breakthrough experiences in our lives are to fall in love and to have a nervous breakdown. Both imply an absence of defenses and an energy that wants to be released. In the latter case, our culture pathologizes this energy, drugs it, shocks it, and closes it down. Falling in love, which is more socially acceptable, is having such an affinity for someone, some idea, or some passion, that the obstacles to intimacy are dissolved. Love gives us the opportunity to get out of the way, to let go of whatever holds us back. Classical psychotherapy would call this "ego death." Teilhard de Chardin describes this as shattering our mental categories, transforming how we see the world internally. Dom Helder Camara shows us another route to such a breakthrough when he counsels, "Accept surprises that upset your plans." In other words, let go.

The process of letting go is catalyzed by events in our lives. It is a spiritual strategy for dealing with pain, disappointment, and all the bitter and burdensome events that are part and parcel of our lives.

The opposite of letting go is thinking that we have all the answers, that we have a predetermined plan for our lives, that we've got it all figured out ahead of time. Letting go means that the creative energy of the divine is allowed expression within and through us. It's like being on a sailboat when the wind comes up and allowing it to take the boat on a new course. That wind takes us to a place we could never have discovered on our own. When our mental categories shatter in such a way, we can feel the turbulence inside. The way we saw the world is challenged and reorganized.

Another dimension of the letting go process is coming to terms with the fact that we are divine but not God. Divinization is not equivalent to being God. Letting go means moving from narcissism to mysticism.

Narcissism is when we're centered on ourselves in our inordinate psychic introspection. Everything is us. The world circles around us. Mysticism is cosmic-centered: it is a oneness with all that is. Gratitude means we let go of the sense that we have an inherent right to be, and begin to see life as a gift. This is a major and necessary shift if we are to grow spiritually.

We also have to let go of the belief that we are unhealable. One reason there is so much therapy is that we don't believe it works. We often use therapy to convince ourselves that only a miracle could cure us. This flows from the misguided conception, implied in the idea of original sin, that we are unhealable. Part of the process of letting go is forgiving ourselves, acknowledging our original goodness, and realizing we are still inherently good.

Letting go is also about forgiving others. Forgiving those who have offended us is letting go of the enemy.

And what about letting go of a dull life or one lived only in memory? I had a friend who was a hospice nurse. When she talked to her patients, many of whom had cancer, she would ask, "How has cancer blessed your life?" The stories of gratitude she heard were amazing. On some deep level, we know that whatever happens, it redounds to good. Think of your own stories of grief and loss and letting go, whether it was with a spouse, a relationship, an occupation, or an illness. At one moment, it felt devastating, and it was, but ultimately something new shined through those moments. It's part of the human journey, the act of surrender and letting go. Meister Eckhart says it this way: "God is not found in the soul by adding anything, but by a process of subtraction."

When I was a little boy in Ontario, we had a pear tree in the backyard. My father would prune it, and after he cut some of the branches off, the poor thing looked rather withered and unspectacular. But then the next year, guess what? Bigger pears! Juicier pears. We grow our soul just like that pear tree. When things somehow are or appear to be taken from us, it creates the opportunity for something new to come through. It is a great paradox, but it is profound and always present. The soul grows by subtraction. That's worth meditating on.

Remembering

Storytelling is at the center of the spiritual journey. Remembering is about story-ing. Jack Shea is a great storyteller; he said that if you feel consoled, inspired, and healed by stories, it's because they have connected you with the loving vitality of soul. Therefore, one way to grow your soul is to tell your story. Reflect on your story. When you gather with groups, in wisdom circles, tell the stories of your ancestors, the stories of your grandkids or your children or your communities, the stories of your tradition, the stories of the universe. Tell the stories of all the things you hold dear.

Stories are the way we connect with each other. Every tradition uses stories as a vehicle for communication. We tell stories as a way of identifying who we are. Our culture also has stories, as does our universe.

Our lives can be viewed from three perspectives: the personal, the cultural, and the cosmic. The stories we're writing about ourselves, the story of society, and the story of the universe are all one story. One of the major insights of our time is that our lives are chapters in the big story.

When you get to know somebody, you want to hear their story. You want to know where that person came from, what their origins are, where they have been. From that, you might have some idea where they are at this moment and who they are.

We discover our own identity through storytelling. Classic psychotherapy is storytelling. Therapy is changing our personal story from one of woundology to one of original goodness. That is the process of healing. In cosmology, we locate our story within the larger universe.

A story energizes us. There's something about being able to tell our story that heals us, that makes pain more bearable.

The spiritual practice of storytelling is the practice of remembering. You can't tell a story without a memory. Stories reveal changes and transformational moments. The shifts that happen over time are incorporated into our stories. Self-reflective consciousness is the unique gift of humanity. We are the universe reflecting on itself. When we tell our stories, we are also speaking on behalf of Earth.

Richard Harmon of the Industrial Areas Foundation NW Regional Office in Portland, Oregon, said, "When we speak from the center of our sacredness, Earth in its pain and tenderness is speaking through us."

Stories are a way that we achieve meaning. Thomas King, the Canadian writer and broadcast presenter who often writes about First Nations, said, "There are no truths. Only stories." When we tell stories and see the universe as a story, we are remembering the series of transformational events that appear over time, out of which this present moment evolves.

When we tell someone our story, we speak of defining moments. Thomas Berry would call these "moments of grace"—the gifts of opportunity when transformation is possible. Story is a way to access and express these moments of transformation. A story also knits together our inner fragmentation and then connects us to others so that we don't feel alone.

Our story is a dimension of the universe story. The story of the universe can be understood in four chapters: the galactic period from the flaring forth and formation of the elements; the formation of Earth itself; the beginning-of-life period, when plants and animals emerged; and our chapter, the human period, marked by the rise of culture and consciousness.

Though in our culture we tend to think of story as something written down in a book, something communicated exclusively with words, the stories we are talking about are broader than that. The birds tell the story, the sun tells the story, the music, the breeze. Stories are communicated on many levels: sound and smell and image and light and darkness.

Thomas Berry said we explain things by telling their story: how they came into being and the changes that have taken place over time. Each person is a story unfolding in time, and so is the universe, whose story began unfolding about thirteen billion years ago.

Every story is revelation. The divine is communicated to us through story. Our culture tends to have a narrow vision of revelation, confining it to the canonical scriptures and the time before the death of the last apostle. Revelation is boxed in. In the cosmological view, revelation happens daily, moment by moment. It's happening right now. It's always unfolding. Implications of that story are that everything is valuable, that all dimensions of life should be represented in any decision-making process, that the divine is present everywhere, that diversity is something to celebrate and not repress.

Practicing Compassion

Compassion is being in an equal relationship with those in need, whether human or other-than-human. Compassion is not doing something for someone to make them feel inferior. Meister Eckhart said, "The soul is where God works compassion." We grow our soul by the practice of compassion. Eckhart also said the best name for God is compassion.

My image of compassion is that of a mother embracing her child, holding her close while being willing to let go when the time comes. This reminds me of the divine embrace of the universe, which I see as a curvature of compassion. We live in the arms of a universe, where there is a balance between the forces of expansion and gravity. If either element were out of balance, our universe would not exist. The point of harmony is an expression of the curvature of compassion. This key reality of our universe—that our life depends on achieving equilibrium—is reflected in many aspects of human life, such as our striving to balance our need for both continuity and discontinuity, or innovation and tradition, in healthy ways. We need continuity with our roots, but we also need to live in this moment, making the tradition present and palpable today. Reflecting on the image of the divine curvature of compassion gives us insight, strength, and compassion as we work to change the structures and worldview that have become desacralized.

The practice of compassion is always to be in relationship with the *anawim*, those "little ones without a voice." All of us feel at times like we are members of the anawim in our churches and in our society. Finding the compassionate curve that results from embracing each other while mining the gold underneath the crust of our traditions is what will nurture our lives.

"Compassion" is another word for "belonging." It is a reciprocal relationship with the anawim. Belonging is a source of revelation, through our relationship with the other, with deep listening, we hear the voice of God and contact the divine. Belonging brings a fuller realization of our connection to the universe, to home, and to our place in the cosmos.

In hope, commitment, community, celebration, creativity, transcendence, and compassion we experience the life of our tradition.

Mother's Day Prayer

You gave us love.
You gave us life.
You gave us family and friends.
Today we celebrate
how you bring beauty to each of us
through the flowering forth
of hibiscus, rose, gardenia, and daisy.
Happy Mother's Day to all mothers.

A New Vision of Belonging

We have a longing to become more conscious and more compassionate. To realize this vision, we allow the creative process to unfold in our lives so we can give birth to the most authentic expression of ourselves. We increase our receptivity to new ideas and new ways of acting; dare to embrace the future, with an openness to difference and a sense of adventure; and regard change with a sense of anticipation. We develop a reverence for the wisdom figures of yesterday and today: our ancestors, our elders, and those of our tradition who have become architects for a prophetic and mystical life.

As we develop a mystical and engaged cosmology of intimacy and contemplation and become increasingly open to the longing of our heart, we grow in the conviction that each person is genetically coded for goodness and compassion. We have an increased ability to integrate spirituality and good work. We honor creativity and bring beauty and healing to the poor and suffering of the world. We simplify our lives, increase our commitment to justice, and expand our understanding of belonging.

Belonging is not a destination. Indeed, it spurs us on to new longings. One belonging leads to another, and another. Belonging moves us forward, deepens us, lures us into ever more profound experiences of belonging. Belonging is a process of mutuality. What we belong to also belongs to us. There is reciprocity in belonging, a oneness and unity. *Belonging* can be another word for mysticism. Ultimate belonging is experienced in our relationship with the divine. The poets and the prophets of the past and present talk about a restlessness, an incompleteness, and an intense thirst quenchable only by a relationship with the divine. This is the ultimate homecoming, the ultimate belonging.

One of the symptoms of our current dysfunctional cosmology is a sense of homelessness. I believe that, because on a deep psychic level, we are unable to come home to our planet, we have been unable to heal the wound of homelessness that ravages our country. When we fall in love with our planet and the planetary community, we can extend our concern beyond ourselves to a culture of belonging—for the planet, for the people, for the plants, the animals, and all expressions of life.

Each of the classical traditions points us to a place of ultimate belonging: nirvana, heaven, paradise, a state of mystical union. *Realized eschatology* is a theological term for letting heaven happen now, for making the future present in our midst in this moment. Science reveals that we live in a web of relationship, and that the cosmos itself is a place of belonging. This web of relationship is a pattern that connects us all. Belonging can heal the despair that stalks our culture and diminishes hope. When hope springs up in the soul, we become connected with life, with Earth, and the divine.

There is a connection between longing, belonging, and chaos. The absence of belonging is longing. When we're in a state of longing, we're off-balance because we're reaching for something—for a connection, a relationship, something to ground us, to root us. This chaotic state is uncomfortable and essential for change. The chaotic state is really the precursor of something opening up for us, to take us to another level, another place, another journey.

The longing or the be-longing we experience is the capacity to deal with internal dislocation and the uncertainty about our traditions, our communities, and our lives. This uncertainty can be the energetic force that moves us to a new state of coherence. Change won't happen without dislocation: cultural dislocation, intrapsychic dislocation, relational dislocation. This new territory is often disturbing, dangerous, and challenging.

It is also refreshing, inviting, and new; chaos is often the threshold to belonging. The capacity to embrace the instability of our existence, to hold it in community with friends, in our meditative reflective times, in our bodies, and in our traditions and in our prayer gives us the capacity to belong deeply in new ways. This movement toward belonging is beginning to happen.

Everyone, Everything Belongs

The new story and the cosmology that flows from it remind us that everything belongs in the universe. Scientist David Bohm is famous for saying that physical reality is not a collection of separate objects but rather is an undivided whole. There might be sociological and cultural evidence of separateness, but no scientific evidence. If we can allow the cosmology to truly seep into us, if we can meditate on belonging in the universe, we will experience belonging.

Fritjoff Capra and David Steindl-Rast wrote a book entitled *Belonging in the Universe*. From their perspective, everything belongs. All of us belong. The trees belong. The puppies belong. The worms belong. The rain belongs. Everything is related and interconnected.

Consider the following situations about not belonging. Take a few moments to reflect on what these questions evoke in you. You may choose to write, or draw, or sing as you ponder.

- Have you ever been in a country where you felt you didn't belong?
- Have you had an experience because of your ethnicity or your family history where you felt you did not belong?
- Have you been confronted with a political situation where you felt alienated or at odds with those in power?
- Have you ever felt rooted in your own tradition and yet felt you did not belong within that tradition?

- Have you ever felt that, because of your gender, you did not belong?

Now consider times when you did belong:

- Have you ever felt a sense of belonging through friendship?
- Have you felt a connection with the divine, God, source, spirit?
- Have you ever felt you belonged to God?
- Have you ever felt you belonged to your body, that you felt embodied, that you and your body belong to one another?
- Have you ever felt in your communities or educational experiences a sense of community and belonging?
- Have you ever felt there was real meaning and purpose in your life, and that you belonged to a sense of destiny about your existence?

As you complete your reflection, focus briefly on two final questions:

- Where did you feel most strongly that you belonged?
- What remains your greatest challenge?

Belonging happens when the longing of soul, life, Earth, and the divine are quenched and responded to. Belonging happens when we are able to integrate intimacy and contemplation, communion and solitude, inwardness and the prophetic struggle, politics and mysticism, inner work and the analytical mind, soul work and community action, connection and interdependence, listening and recognition. At the edge of our longing, we discover a mystical and engaged cosmology to guide us into the days ahead.

The Voice of Our Calling

There is an enduring tension between belonging and the authentic self. One way of exploring this question is to trust in quantum leaps. There's a risk involved, of course—that is what is meant by a "quantum leap." There's a time between departure and landing when one feels unsure whether there are any "air-traffic controllers" monitoring our leap. And yet it's thrilling when we burst out as our authentic self and find ourselves genuinely accepted, perhaps for the very first time.

To begin to live authentically from a functional cosmology requires that we experience a period of dislocation from the dominant culture. In other words, to live the new cosmology makes us less able to function in our dysfunctional world. To create a new world require courage and commitment as we live in this world while simultaneously striving to change it. It will also require new structures of support during these in-between times.

Relating to the Little Ones

I met a young man named Mark a few years ago who seemed to radiate goodness. His mother told me that when he was applying to the university for admission to a graduate program, he wrote the mandatory essay, which was a major part of determining whether or not he would be accepted, about his dog, Maxie. The essay could have been a daunting task, but Mark took his dog with him into it and did just fine. His story suggests to me that being close to a little one, whether a child or an animal, is a way of accessing our connection to God. It is a way to deal with our fears. It is a way to grow our soul. Somehow, the image of the divine is often revealed to us more clearly through the unprotected and the un-powerful.

The young need meaning and beauty to awaken to their place in life and the search for fulfillment. In our reflection on the place of the little ones, we hear a clarion call for their dignity, identity, security, and peace.

Making Authentic Rituals

Ritual is the language of the soul. Why do we have ritual? Because we need symbolic language to express the deeper recesses of our hearts and minds and souls, to connect the conscious to the unconscious. There are cultural rituals inspired by a spiritual impulse, such as protests to demand tougher gun laws, rallies for climate justice, and demonstrations supporting Black Lives Matter. Rabbi Heschel says, "Prayer is meaningless unless it is subversive."

Eucharists don't all happen in churches. On one Holy Thursday, I was privileged to be with a group of people in San Francisco in the Tenderloin. Mary Ann Finch worked there with a group called Care Through Touch Institute. We were celebrating Holy Thursday by practicing the gospel mandate of Jesus to wash the feet of the poor as an act of service and generosity and inclusion. We went around in groups and massaged the feet of the homeless as a gesture of service. It was incredibly joyful.

Touching these people's feet often turned on fifty years of story. It just poured out of them. One woman said her marriage was broken and she hadn't seen her family for years. She had written to all her granddaughters in Massachusetts, but only one answered her. She went upstairs to the little room she lived in and brought down the letter to show me. It said, "Dear Grandma, I have your picture on my desk, and when I do my homework, I look at you and I love you." That meant a lot to her. Even though her other grandchildren didn't answer, she was joyful because one did. In this ritual, we both grew our souls, and that act of service was Eucharist; together we reenacted the Last

Supper. Communion was happening. As Miriam Therese Winter said, "There's little-e eucharist and there's big-E Eucharist. Little-e eucharist happens when we communicate, not necessarily only when we commune." And it happens a lot.

Prayer is the movement from illusion to reality. It's less about changing God's mind than about embracing the reality of our own lives.

Celebrating Creativity

The imagination is at the heart of being fully human. Eckhart says, "If you have sorrow in your heart, you're not yet a mother; you're still on the way to giving birth." What he meant by that is that there's a sense of dis-ease if we're not being creative, a feeling that something isn't right with us.

Creativity is not dualistic. It's not objectifying. It is a mystical experience of being one with the clay, the painting, or the dance. There is an art gallery in Kleinburg, just north of Toronto, that houses the work of the Group of Seven. One of these Canadian artists, Lawren Harris, has painted wonderful sunsets and sunrises. Somebody once asked him, "Lawren, what does it mean for you to be creative?" He said, "When I paint, I try to get to the summit of my soul. I paint from there, where the universe sings."

Creativity is at the heart of us. It is about giving expression to what lies deep within our hearts. You can do this in a conversation with your spouse. You can do it in your work, with your children, with your colleagues, in your community. Creativity is not limited to a paintbrush or to being in a studio. It enlivens the studio of our lives, where we create and recreate life itself.

We are never more like God than when we are creating. Each individual is unique, a reflection of the divine, and our acts of creation enhance the likeness. A scientist I know in British Columbia was working on a complicated theorem. A creative person looked at the problem and gave him the answer. However, it was ten years before the scientist was able to work out the equations. The imagination precedes the intellect, always.

Using our imagination and allowing our creative heart to itself themselves in all areas of our lives grows our souls.

Honoring the Beauty of Creation

To experience the beauty of creation is to have a sacramental consciousness by which we recognize the face of God in all of nature. This is another kind of literacy that all of us are capable of, though sometimes not conscious of, when we read God's face in a sunrise or sunset, a bluebonnet flower, a storm, a mountain range, a prairie, an ocean. These are the moments when creation speaks to us and tells us the story of the universe. St. Bernard wrote, "You will find more lessons in the woods than in books. Trees and stones will teach you what you cannot learn from masters." Jim Couture, a graduate of the Sophia Center program, wrote, "The cavity of our souls needs to be filled with the wonder and awe of the natural world." We grow our soul every time we respond to such beauty.

Breath

Across the Maritimes today
and in the forests beyond,
I hear a breathless cry:
I can't breathe!
This, the plea of George Floyd,
murdered on the street
three years ago.
And now, on this early May day,
the plea of our planet.
Smoke fills the orange sky,
obliterates the sun,
poisons the atmosphere.
People wipe their burning eyes,
walk the empty streets.
Listen as they cry out,
I can't breathe, I can't breathe!

Envisioning

To grow our soul, we need to have hope, a vision, and a dream of what our life could be. There's nothing sadder than a life spent just going through the motions. A lot of people are going through the motions, just hanging in there, always waiting, never taking the initiative. For them, life has no deep meaning. We need a vision to keep hope alive and to lead us to seek an answer for Mary Oliver's question: "What is it you plan to do with your one wild and precious life?"

It takes a vision and a dream to draw you forward, to help you attend to that still-small voice within, and to discern the truth in what you hear from the pulpit, your colleagues, your spouse, your children, your puppy. At some moment, the shape of your future will become clearer and you will identify and claim the visions that were yours when you were born. Yours will not be an unlived life.

We can also grow our soul to recognize and respect the sacredness and depth in what might seem to be unlikely places. A group called the Community Action Network (CAN) in Dublin works with people who are homeless and suffer from domestic violence, addiction, unemployment, and other forms of human pathos that are so prevalent.

When CAN members get together, they ask people to go out and walk in the streets of the city. Their one requirement is that you walk with your "soul eyes" open. Soul eyes allow a person to see the sacredness and depth in all they encounter on their walk.

When the members of this group return, they report seeing syringes on the street, a flower bursting forth in a garden, an unhoused person, a child, the rain—they see everything that they encounter with new compassion and clarity.

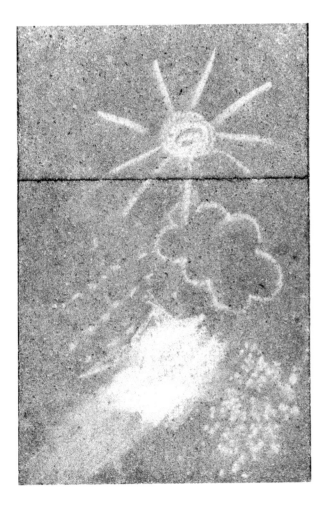

The Spirit Speaks

The spirit stirs.
Words well up;
they speak for themselves
of many things,
of sacred turbulence,
of wonder and surprise,
of awesome beauty,
and the deepest aspirations of the heart.
Beauty beckons us
to suffer and rejoice,
to allow the paradox of presence,
to engage us all.
And from agony and ecstasy,
to see uniqueness born.
This is my surprise to you.
This is my true joy.
That beauty will be born
and that all you hope for will make you free.

Soul Work, Prayer, Spiritual Practice

Soul work moves us from illusion to reality. It is less about petition and contrition than about attuning our lives and minds to the unfolding dynamics of the universe.

Soul work is an encounter with beauty and pain, an expression of gratitude, a search for meaning, a language that transcends all traditions.

In soul work, we contact the pulsating, originating energy of the universe. Through receptivity and response, we dive deeply into the joys and sorrows of life, and experience the solidarity of engagement.

Soul work and spiritual practice are an attitude of the heart, an openness to the meaning of existence. Through soul work, we gain perspective on God's action in the world.

In our spiritual practice, we realize that challenge, fear, gratitude, hope for possibilities, and tendencies toward self-destruction are present in all people. We discover that life's mysteries are present in everyone. Our spiritual practice emerges from our deepest intuitions and is understood as universal for everyone. Sound spiritual practice is dialectical (e.g., progressive and conservative, innovative and traditional).

Soul work celebrates the dramatic moments of creativity and new life. We name the human journey within the context of the paschal mystery, and intensify the mystery and name in everyday existence. We are continuously reminded that tomorrow can be different than today, that our deepest longings have a cosmic and sacred source.

Prayer happens through our interaction with others. It is here that we discover who we are. It is here that revelation happens. Through our engagements, we choose again and again the path to transformation and discover that life on Earth is possible.

Soul work happens in stillness. In transparent moments, we perceive the universe. We experience gratitude and joy, validity and purpose, and we become energized for the journey toward meaning and fulfillment.

In our soul work, we enhance our visual literacy and discover a language of the soul, a language that speaks of popular piety, veranda narratives, and vocational destiny.

Our soul work includes silent recollection and engaged action, a vulnerability to wonder, an invitation to mystery, an openness to reverence, an experience of belonging, and an awareness of the sacredness of life.

Soul work provides access to identity and reveals our place in the community of life.

Our spiritual practice involves dialogue, listening, communal ritual, and critical reflection. Spiritual practice activates a radical response to life, and a moral embrace of the three commandments of creation:

- Celebrate difference and honor creativity.
- Nurture communion and express compassion.
- Revere depth and the soul of all sentient beings.

Threshold Moments

Find my voice.
Respond to the impulse that lies deep within.
Live at the threshold and precipice of unknowing.
Go beyond the predictability of life.
Stand at the doorway of the unexpected.
Transcend moments of restlessness and compulsion.
Embrace the revelatory moment.
Stand still, enveloped in the solitude of existence.
Discover what it means to be free,
Irrigate the soul
and embrace the fault lines of your heart.

Contemplation and Soul: Action/Reflection

How is your heart opened and your soul stirred as you contemplate the awe and wonder of the universe and the galaxies of your soul?

In what ways has the experience of intimacy and solitude enhanced your capacity to give full and conscious attention to your experience of ultimate mystery?

How through moments of contemplation, trusting your body, being willing to engage with others, and embracing the present moment, have you been able to overcome the fear that blocks your capacity to experience the inmost recesses of your soul and to find your place in community?

What actions will energize and enhance your capacity to respond to the longing for intimacy and contemplation that resides in the universe and in your own soul?

To truly discover who we really are, we must engage in a search:

- For a sacrament of engagement, where our work for equality and justice becomes an act of love
- For the subtle presence of the divine, who, as we discover with our new awareness, is already there
- For a new sensitivity to the poor and oppressed, whose vulnerability somehow reveals a transparency that allows the divine presence to shine through
- To penetrate and transform the negative energy and bitterness that look like justice and are so often present in the struggle

- To extend our internal sensitivity beyond self to embrace the other and Earth
- To savor silence and discover there increased clarity, focus, and self-esteem
- To discover the currents of deep inner wisdom that foster our attentiveness to dreams, imagination, and the unspoken language of God
- For increased energy in the struggle, an enhanced sense of community, and the time to explore a greater sense of purpose
- For a deeper meaning of animateur, as soul workers who are willing to risk, slow down, go deeper, light a candle to dispel the darkness, and bring beauty back to the world
- For an increased capacity to live with mystery, with the sense of not knowing, and to find a resilient spirit even in broken dreams, loneliness, and the massive bureaucracy that often clouds our work
- For our generational task, to discover soul in the great work as we listen attentively to the little ones of God and discover there a mystical cosmology that will nurture engagement and a culture of hope

AT THE EDGE OF OUR LONGING

Part 2
Longing of Life

A Canticle to Life

We awaken, as if for the first time, to life as primary sacrament:

To a new life of cosmology, ecology, community, and wisdom.

To a life of reciprocity, gratefulness, and awe.

To a life of cosmic common vision, creativity, and reverence.

To a life of natural beauty, mysticism, and opportunity for the great work and integral presence.

To a life that is holistic, that sees with new eyes the divine goodness everywhere.

To a life where education is a spiritual practice that celebrates both intimacy and contemplation.

To a life where we witness and therefore become.

To a life whose culture is being brought to a boil in and through the cosmological imagination that bursts forth from the heart of humanity and the heart of the cosmos itself.

To a world of gratitude for good companions on the way and for the awakening hunger for life that resides in the hearts of the young.

To a new world that we can call home, a vision that will energize the next generation so we can become a people of gratitude and glory for all that has been, is, and will be.

In this new life:

We will marry mind and the soul, the cognitive and the moral.

Our hearts and minds will go to the edge of our longing.

We will respond to our unspoken hunger for sacredness and depth.

Together we will give birth to:
A re-enchanted cosmos.
A new liberating cosmology, an operative contextual cosmology.
A new genesis.
A new civilization.
A new moment of grace.
A new paschal moment.
A new sense of destiny founded on a sustainable future, where peace with Earth makes possible peace on Earth in a simultaneous embrace.
A peace that is possible through an enduring journey of courage, joy, celebration, and ecstasy.

Only then can we truly say we are turning enthusiastically for home:
Home to our soul.
Home to life.
Home to Earth.
Home to the divine.

Longing of Liberation

To become vulnerable, to experience deeply, to risk rejection, and to allow our souls to grow with exposure to beauty, wonder, and surprise will bring us more fully to the edge of our longing for life. It is here that our heart cries out in pursuit of life. The poet Rilke writes, "Flare up like a flame and make big shadows I can move in." As defenses melt and our hearts ignite with passion, all that is hidden will emerge. We reach out and open ourselves to relationship, to life. In our vulnerability we embrace paradox, beauty, and terror, and we dance courageously into the depths of self-discovery and life.

A compass guides us on our journey into life. The longing of life explores a new sense of freedom in relationship to class, race, gender, and creation.

We journey with openness and trust into the uncharted future. With gratitude and praise, we celebrate each precious moment, each opportunity to quench our thirst for life. These eternal longings are the compass for the journey that, as Teilhard de Chardin puts it, we "dare to call our life." This interior compass guides us forward into the depths of our emotional truth. A compass, unlike a map that already has the destination marked out, continues to guide us through an ever-changing and unfolding journey.

Our quest for life, for freedom, involves taking on a new identity, becoming a new species. From this perspective, our focus is not only the liberation of humanity but the liberation of life itself. We take up the challenge of a preferential option for the poor and the poor Earth.

A New Meaning for a Listening Heart

My brother phoned. He had received the results of his catheterization, and the diagnosis was not good: he would be undergoing triple-bypass surgery in the morning.

As we talked, questions, fear, and memories tumbled into my consciousness. I was transported back to my adolescence and recalled with stark vividness the desolation I felt at my mother's funeral. As my brother spoke of his possible death, I felt the buffer between myself and mortality torn away. And when he asked to "talk to me about something spiritual," my sense of inadequacy reached a high peak.

We spoke that evening about questions of pain, suffering, death, prayer, and personal conscience. It was the most intimate and meaningful exchange in all our decades of life. On the eve of open-heart surgery, my brother's heart opened as never before. Long before the surgeon's incision, he was changed. Time, children, marriage, and the preciousness of existence swelled with greater value. It was a powerful lesson for the entire family: when we face death, we embrace life.

As I pondered these life-changing events, I recalled the wisdom of Saul Alinsky, the architect of community organization, who decades ago reminded us that when we have a heart attack or some other serious illness, our values change, and what seemed important before does not matter now. He saw the acceptance of our own mortality as the prerequisite for living with a fresh sense of wonder.

With my brother's post-operative prognosis good, and his recovery well underway, his children, siblings, and spouse were left to reflect on the lessons that lie on the threshold of death. The card I sent to him immediately after his surgery had the following words: "Friends who plant kindness gather love." Inside I wrote:

> *Dear Bob,*
> *This card says it all. These days have reminded us of how precious you are and how precious life is. The next stage of your journey will be richer, deeper, and more joyful. Thank you for your courage and your life. I'm glad you're well.*
> *Love,*
> *Jim*

As I distilled the wisdom from those turbulent days, I realized, perhaps for the first time, that to encounter mortality is to begin life anew.

The Brazilian educator Paulo Freire wrote, 'The space of the democratic-minded teacher who learns to speak by listening is interrupted by the intermittent silence of his or her own capacity to listen, waiting for that voice that may desire to speak from the depths of its own silent listening." The willingness to listen, to learn, to change, to be vulnerable, to engage deeply with the emanation of one's or another's heart is at the center of our longings. Silence makes it possible to be committed to the experience of communication, to hear the questions, the doubt, the creativity of the person who is speaking and to discover our own voice.

Listening and recognition are the greatest gifts we can give to another and also to ourselves. Their practice invites intimacy, makes communication possible, energizes the spirit, and creates a context of fertile silence to foster wisdom. To listen is a permanent attitude of being open to the word of the other, to the gesture of the other, to the difference of the other.

Listening requires a generous, loving heart; respect; tolerance; humility; joy; love; and openness to what is new, to what is welcome, to change, to perseverance, to struggle, to hope, and to justice. Listening gives access to what is eternally true, to the heart of wisdom, of liberation, of creation. It flows from a conviction that life is ours to create. By listening, we can satisfy the longing for intimacy, the cravings of our soul for life.

A Passion for Justice

It was eleven o'clock on a Chicago morning in May 2001. The funeral mass for Monsignor John J. Egan had just concluded, and the procession would soon be on its way to the cemetery. Though I was in Berkeley, I found myself imagining standing there on the sidewalk, surrounded by many who had loved and learned from him, remembering with deep feelings of gratitude and loss the great man who had left us.

I had met Jack Egan at Notre Dame more than three decades before. As I sat in his office that day wondering about my future, the telephone rang often. On the line were people from the justice community of the American Catholic Church, such as Dan Berrigan, Gino Baroni, Dorothy Day, Kathy Kelly, and Margie Tuite. Each had a personal connection to the man Andrew Greeley called "the midwife of every significant Catholic Action initiative in our era."

Jack became a friend and advocate, a person whose sensitivity to the needs of the poor and powerless boiled over into a passionate commitment to justice and civil rights for all. Jack had the capacity to make you feel like you belonged. He spread his gospel of "information, support, and the possibility of common action" to all who were asea in the turbulent years of the post-Vatican II church. He was ahead of his time, behind every issue that hoped for and promised justice. He was sensitive, even easily hurt, yet profoundly attuned to the pain of the marginalized, to those who have no voice.

Tim Unsworth captured the essence of Monsignor Egan in his book *The Last Priests in America: Conversations with Remarkable Men*: "Jack Egan remains the consummate communicator. He is the master of the short but pointed letter and the perfectly aimed phone call." It is for his passion for justice that I remember him most—a passion that made a difference in my life and the lives of many. I also remember his personal kindness and support when I really needed it.

He spent time with me at Notre Dame University when I flew in unexpectedly for a visit. He wrote to the bishop to express his support for my ministry. He made it possible for me to participate in the Urban Training Center for Christian Mission and the Industrial Areas Foundation Saul Alinsky Training Institute in Chicago, both pivotal experiences for me. He invited me onto the board of the Catholic Committee on Urban Ministry and supported my work as Canadian liaison.

Most of all, he believed in people and made it possible for us to believe in ourselves. He was a good man, a good friend, a good priest. I still miss him.

Dinner with Donna at Christmas

It was Christmas morning in Brielle, New Jersey. Outside, the winds sent blistering sheets of rain across the windows and into the streets. Snow was promised by the forecasters, as people in this village on the Jersey shore and other coast-side towns prepared to stay inside, away from winter's fury on this day on which we celebrate a child's birth.

The doorbell rang. My sister and I welcomed my sister's friend Fran and her friend Donna to our newly formed Christmas day community. Fran was a volunteer who worked with those who have developmental disabilities. She had chosen to share the holiday with Donna, a developmentally challenged adult, and with us.

Donna's presence among us turned out to be a gift, an unexpected incarnation on that nativity morning, encouraging us to reflect in a new way on the meaning of the day and what it is that we, in fact, celebrate on Christmas.

As I entered into Donna's obvious enjoyment of her Christmas lunch, I found myself musing on Christmas and its meaning for Donna, myself, and others in the twenty-first century. I understood the incarnation as the interface between divinity and creation, spirit and matter, humanity and the other-than-human world. It was the birth of a child; the unfolding of a flower; and the genesis of an insight, project, or community like ours around the holiday table.

On that Christmas day in New Jersey, as the rain turned to snow, the meal was completed. In the companionable silence that followed, I heard whispers about the birth of newness. Once again, incarnation happened, divinity was present, and the Earth community vibrated with new life.

Donna gathered her presents of clothes, candy, and cards, and with happy smiles, took her leave to be driven home by Fran. As they vanished into the night, I was conscious of my own wounds and weaknesses, sometimes more hidden than our guest's. The meaning of Christmas seemed clearer. Divinity had visited us in the person of a woman, Donna, whose very wounds and uncomplicated wisdom were the manger of newness on that incarnation day.

At This Moment

At this moment,
I straddle the intersections of life
and choose at this crossroad of existence,
to endure the pain of dislocation
and be freed from the conformity of trodden paths.
May the guiding star of tomorrow
promise to illuminate the sky,
access the wisdom of a child,
now healed from denial and despair,
to once again relentlessly pursue
a deeper purpose and
avoid becoming marooned
in an as-yet-unlived life.

Tell Me About Yourself

A new room, new friends
and also the same familiar questions:
Who am I? Why am I here? What am I here to do?

So I say, "Tell me about yourself."
About how you were present
when the universe was born,
about that supernova amazement of your soul.
About your mother, the one who gave you life.
Tell me about the journey you are on,
the promptings of your soul,
the compass that guides your life.

Together, let's share our hopes and dreams,
find unfamiliar answers to old questions
on the winding road that lies ahead.

Bethlehem Needs to Happen

Bethlehem needs to happen
Through the welcoming of world religions into a unity of planetary peace.

In the celebration of science, art, and mysticism, to recover a new origin story for our lives.

Through radical listening and storytelling, so that we may come home to the rich soil of our psyches.

That we may recover the wisdom of a theology of the incarnation and may find in the differentiated unity of the trinity, a basis for reverence and love.

That we may find in the liberating practices of cultural work, primary actions for freedom and geo-justice making.

In places of worship, so healing can come to our bodies, to our imaginations, and to our authentic desire to create, through the arts and the art of prayer, the art of our lives.

In hospital emergency rooms and outpatient clinics, so welcoming can happen and compassion can be born.

In school classrooms so that feelings, intuitions, and ideas can commune, and holistic learning can take place.

So that capitalism can be healed of its competition, and social policy can recover a sensitivity to spirit.

So that acquisitiveness and lifestyles of apparent necessity can give way to simplicity and a reverential use of energy.

So that gatherings and communities can respect differences, while individuals and outsiders can be welcomed into the fabric of support and solution.

So that spring can continually be born of winter.

That the seasons of Earth can also be the seasons of our heart.

That we may reverence creation for its own sake, and in fields of plenty, grow bread for a hungry world.

In libraries, in institutes for cancer and AIDS research, in detox centers, and in places of hospitality for the poor and lonely.

Where waters are poisoned, Earth is pummeled with fertilizers, and the air is rancid with acid rain.

When the aspirations of youth are crushed by cynicism and the wisdom of age is discarded and repressed.

So that we can see in the incarnation of Christmas—an event that continues today, a genesis that continues to happen in our cosmos, in our psyches, and in our souls—an incarnation story of our time, a story emerging from the heart of oneness.

Gospel of the Moment

We ask ourselves, "How can we peer through the darkness of smoke, of violence, of fear, of greed, of devastation and death, and find there a light of hope and rebirth to illuminate our perspective on war and the pain and destruction that accompany it?"

With this question in mind, I remember the promise of Oscar Romero, who proclaimed, "If they kill me, I will rise in the people of El Salvador."

And I recall the words of German theologian Johannes Metz, who reflecting on the legacy of his country, wrote, "For me, doing theology meant doing theology in the face of Auschwitz, in the face of the Holocaust (and though this holds good in a very special way for Christians and theologians in Germany, it does not apply to them exclusively; for the Holocaust is not just a German catastrophe, but on closer inspection, a Christian catastrophe). I began to ask myself: What sort of theology can one do with one's back to Auschwitz— before the impending catastrophe, during the catastrophe, after the catastrophe of Auschwitz." In the same way, today we cannot operate with our backs to the current turbulence and threats to our basic democratic values and the well-being of our planet.

The gospel of the moment calls upon us to both read scripture and to be aware of the state of the world and to respond in a reflective and transformative way. This gospel of the moment process begins with a community of self-aware people who hold an evolutionary worldview in which each person wakes up to an entirely new world each day. It is a world in which we pursue our true destiny. Empowered by companionship and the ability to act, we move forward to more fully realize what is possible.

I picture the future as a planetary Pentecost. In the Christian tradition, Pentecost was the birth of the church—the birth of a new community of relationships and new life. In England, toward the end of the Second World War, Vera Lynn popularized a song called "When the Lights Go On Again All Over the World." At the time, people were terrified that lights would make their homes targets for bombers. I suggest that it is time to turn the lights on—the lights of creativity and compassion, the lights of relationship and hope, the lights of a new awakening community.

We need to look at the relationship between intimacy and contemplation. In popular culture as well as in our personal lives, there is probably a lack of one of these. We need both intimacy, so that our soul doesn't dry up, and enough silence and contemplative time in which to grow our soul. Edward Schillebeeckx, OP, described this dynamic when he said, "Without mysticism, politics soon becomes cruel and barbaric, without political love, mysticism becomes sentimental or uncommitted inferiority." If we can balance the two, I think we have the key to a lifestyle that fosters both spiritual development and a peaceful world.

A new mystical and engaged cosmology will reenergize our traditions and make them more relevant. We need cultural as well as personal therapy. We need to *deconstruct* society, to return to our point of origin. Then we need to *reconstruct* our society with the ethical principles that the universe teaches us: to respect differences, honor interiority and inwardness, and promote relationship and community. That is the task of the new cosmology I call *geo-justice*. Taking the dynamics of evolution, putting them into cultural form, and practicing them provides us with a template for justice. The universe teaches us about ethics. If we truly made use of those principles, perhaps we wouldn't need the Ten Commandments. Only then would our vision of tomorrow become one of harmony, balance, and peace.

In-between Times

We gather today only to find
ourselves at in-between times.
You said you were ascending to the Father,
yet you left an absence in my heart.

Today I welcome companions on the journey:
the Indigenous ones who see the divine in all creation,
the feminine mystics who celebrate the inclusiveness of
    life,
the people of science who perceive your presence in all
    that is.

Easter complete, we are ready to welcome Pentecost,
to become one people, one family, one planet, one Earth.
We are companions, no longer separate,
here in these in-between times.

A Eucharist of Compassion

Mary Ann Finch invited us to gather in a circle at the Care Through Touch Institute, a program that provides massage and support for people in the Tenderloin district in San Francisco. As music filled the room, we followed her lead into movement and song. She woke up our bodies so the spirit could also rise.

She reminded me of Dorothy Day, who inspired generations to live lives of voluntary poverty and service to the poor. Mary Ann told us the inner city of San Francisco was her classroom, and her receptive heart a home for those whose lives are "pushed and passed by" by those who, adorned in white shirts, suits, and attaché cases, strive to ignore or escape the gaze of the crucified ones who live in the streets.

In our circle, there was a spirit of joy and playfulness inspired by Mary Ann, who dared to see the suffering Christ in abandoned and displaced people and discovered there a monastery to heal the sacred longings of our cultural soul.

Later, on Holy Thursday, a group of us joined Mary Ann and her colleagues to repeat the generosity of Jesus. Taking his act of service as an example, we massage the feet of the unhoused.

One of the people I was privileged to meet there was the elderly woman originally from Massachusetts, whose story, when I first touched her feet, began to flow from her. It was a story of broken relationships and broken dreams, a lifetime of longing to be accepted and loved.

As we parted, I was grateful for the experience with this woman of the Tenderloin. It was a Eucharist of compassion, a Passover moment for each of us.

On another occasion, a Thanksgiving Day, a group of us joined the Little Brothers of Jesus and Friends of the Elderly to deliver food, drink, and flowers to the elderly people living in single rooms in old hotels. We met people hidden away in their crowded quarters. They were grateful for the gifts we brought and more so for the contact we provided.

Mother of the Streets

I want to know how the child in you longs for home.

When you are frightened or alarmed by people in the streets, remember that a dimension of yourself walks there, lives without an address or documented identity, perhaps spent last night in a cardboard condo in a park, a storefront, or in the rain.

I want you to know that your mother is with you on your journey. She accepts, embraces, loves you, and welcomes you home to her heart.

It is a welcoming heart, a heart of hospitality that feels the pain of unclean needles, the pain of exile and alienation, the pain of rejection by self, other, and the world.

I want you to know that my heart is always open, that my arms embrace you, as my hands offer you bread for the journey. It is the bread of hospitality and nourishment of home.

I want you to know I am present with you in the streets, that you and your lifestyle are as dignified and worthy as are those whose picket fences and gated communities keep out the public, the pain of the people, and also me.

I want you to know that this is a place of connectedness, that this is your home, and that the many relationships of the street bring blessings to your life.

I want you to know that no matter where you are, wherever you sleep, however hopeless you may feel, the street itself is a sacred place, a place for life, a place of nobility, a place of peace where good people and your Mother of the Streets also dwell.

I want you to heal your wound of exile, and I invite you to come home to yourself, to your friends, even to your pain, and of course, to the beautiful person that you are.

I want you to come home—home to the street, home to your God, and home to your Mother of the Streets, who welcomes you.

Reflections at the Edge of Life:
Thoughts on Relatedness

The new story of the universe states that we all come from a common origin. We're related to everything that is; at one with all creation. This universe of which we are a part runs on three principles, which I call derivatives of a living cosmology.

First, there is nothing created that is repetitive. No two things are the same (differentiation). Second, everything is related to everything else (communion). And third, each dimension, whether it is a stone, a cat, a tree, or a human, has an identity that is uniquely its own (interiority).

The heart of a cosmological ethic resides within the practice of these three principles. There's no racism, no sexism, no classism, because we celebrate difference rather than see it as a problem. The universe teaches us that we are not separated, we are in relationship together. Community is necessary for our very survival, as is respect for the uniqueness of each expression of creation.

Trembling

Unable to transform...
despair, powerlessness, early death,
unlived life, desecrated beauty,
alienation, suffering, and pain.

Tremble at the doorway of...
joy, generosity, communion,
and celebrate with newfound freedom
the on-the-spot compassion of energetic hope.

Homeward to Peace

We awaken, as if for the first time,
To the world as primary sacrament.
To a world of cosmology, ecology, community, and wisdom.
To a world of reciprocity, gratefulness, and awe.
To a world of cosmic common vision, creativity, and reverence.
To a world of natural beauty, mysticism, opportunity for the great Work, and integral presence. To a world that is holistic, that sees with new eyes the divine goodness everywhere.
To a world where we witness and therefore become.
To a world of gratitude for good companions on the way.
To the awakening of a hunger for hope that resides in the hearts of the young.
To a new world we can call home, a vision that will energize the next generation so we can become a place of gratitude and glory for all that has been, is, and will be.
It is this new world that will heal our hearts and minds as we go to the edge of our longing.
It is this new world that will respond to the unspoken hunger for sacredness and depth.
It is this new world that will give birth to a new genesis, a new moment of grace, a new Paschal moment.
This new world brings a sense of destiny founded on a sustainable future where peace with Earth makes possible peace on Earth in a simultaneous embrace. This peace is possible through an enduring journey of courage, joy, celebration, and ecstasy. Only then can we truly say we are turning enthusiastically for home: home to our soul, home to life, home to Earth, and home to the divine.

Reimagining Life

I have always been uncomfortable with the presumed dichotomy of "change yourself, then change the world." It is more true to say, "When we change our consciousness, it is inevitable that we also change our actions in the world."

In the world today, the increasing tendency toward fundamentalism impedes our capacity to be open to new challenges and the evolution of thought. It is only through new thought, through a new consciousness, that we will be able to confront the violence and emptiness of our culture and achieve a critical awareness of the multiple oppressions that impinge on our lives and the life of the planet.

Within the depths of our longing for life is the desire for a new humanity and for new ways to care for one another; to celebrate differences of culture, gender, race, and ethnicity; to appreciate beauty; and to live simply, with healthy food and clean water, on this beautiful planet.

Our new humanity will discover that to care for Earth is not just another "issue." We will realize the need to reverse the trends that are extinguishing the lives of many species.

The new human will confront the hierarchical dualism that divides spirit from matter, in which a rank-and-split approach rates pebbles, peaches, poodles, people, angels, and God in order of value. This same value system correlates women with matter and men with spirit, and thereby perpetuates a system of oppression. This system also justifies the plundering of the planet, and by using the language of rape, reveals the link between the oppression of women and the destruction of Earth.

The new human will foster a paradigm of kinship, with all species viewed as neighbors in the community of life. This shift will be accompanied by letting go of the concept of a patriarchal God who is understood as transcendent, remote, and unaffected by the pain of the planet. Alternatively—as has recently been discussed by the Church of England—we will embrace the divine spirit as the gender-neutral face of God, the source that sustains and guides us, knits us together into a single community of life to renew the face of Earth.

The new human will foster a liberating compassion that energizes all things and is in every way on the side of life. As Sr. Helen Prejean, author of *Dead Man Walking*, suggested, we need to recognize that not only the incarcerated but also the health care system, people living in poverty, and Earth itself, are on death row.

As we imagine what it means to be the new human in a continually unfolding universe, we will be called to locate ourselves within a cosmological context and discover the presence of the divine in supernova explosions and the cycles of life.

We will be called to activate a cosmological imagination. Through symbol, intuition, and archetype, we will gain access to the consciousness of the universe, which contains an all-prevailing energy enveloped in emotion, spirit, and love.

The new human will engage in profound shifts of perception and action. Included in these changes will be movement:

- From individualism and competition to community and cooperation
- From anthropocentrism (the human sees mind, pain, and pleasure focused only on the human) to a creation-centered awareness that celebrates sacredness and divine presence in all of life
- From religious sectarianism to a deep ecumenism, with a renewed commitment to one's own tradition, accompanied by an openness to the wisdom of others
- From a divided nationalism to a true patriotism that embraces international cooperation among all nations
- From a narrow self-interest in politics whose sovereignty is vested locally, to a decentralized economic system, to a preferential option for Earth as the best and most benign possibility for planetary peace

As the new human goes to the edge of their longings, our challenge will be to ignite the imagination; mine our heritage; and participate through new and ecological ways, in the democratic process, the education of others, and the practice of green economics.

As we swim like salmon against the stream of the dominant culture, we realize that the ideas and programs that flow from our imagination have unique lives of their own. We see that creativity happens when we are willing to engage opposites; we see that when differences are honored, newness happens. The creation of new life also occurs when the inner life encounters what is outside itself—when the personal and the communal become one. We will contribute to a more gracious and challenging world from the interactions of these apparent opposites.

The interaction between change and continuity will make possible the appearance of something new. It will be nurtured by deep listening to avoid the collision of intercepting dialogues (which occur when each person is planning their response as the other is speaking, and so is not really listening) while making room for the unexpected to emerge. The unexpected in this case is a new culture where divine energy moves freely in people's hearts—a greening spirituality that confronts injustice and retains a radical trust in a future not yet realized.

The new human will be energized by a fresh hope that summons us forward with a newfound courage to participate fully in the creation of a culture in which the poetry of beauty and brokenness will find its realization in a sonnet of justice—a song of compassion that resonates from the heart of the universe and the divine imagination.

Allow Silence

Silence reveals unknown wisdom.
Allow surprises to upset your plans.
Allow this wonderous moment
to be a new beginning.
Allow your heart
to speak of longing
Allow your heart to lead you.
Take my hand and listen with me
as we allow silence to speak to us.

Artists of Life

When cosmologist Brian Thomas Swimme was writing *The Hidden Heart of the Cosmos,* his working title was *The All-Nourishing Abyss.* He meant that nothingness is the source of life, ideas, universe, and creativity. The original fireball—the creative moment that marks the beginning of the universe—cannot be calculated from the very beginning point. There is a time, a mysterious moment, people of faith call the divine creative act. Out of nothingness, in a sense, everything is born.

It's my conviction that the most profound impulse, the most sacred longing of soul that any of us has, is to understand and express our creativity.

Creativity is the impulse inside us that has to find expression. It will do so either in a benevolent way or in a destructive way. Much of the violence in our culture is repressed creativity, as is much of the burnout in our workaday world. Institutional structures are threatened by change and therefore do not encourage creativity.

Creativity, however, is not just one option among many; it's a precondition for an authentic life.

Many people spend the first half of their lives doing things and then the second half of their lives discovering who they are. The problem with such self-discovery occurs when we rely on psychological technologies to tell us who we are. "I'm a 6." "I'm an INFP." "I'm an obsessive-compulsive." I don't think psychological techniques reveal the authentic self.

I'm not saying the Enneagram or Myers-Briggs or other psychological tools aren't valid, but rather that they don't really get to the core of who we are.

The way we discover ourselves is through the creative act, not through a psychological technology.

Creativity takes courage. Anastasia MacDonald, a Sophia Center graduate and my work-study student while I was preparing a manuscript, coined a word: *creageous.* She combined *courage* and *creativity* into one word. The prophets of today are people of courage and creativity. They are the saints of tomorrow and are often exiled in their own time.

Anastasia wrote a poem expanding on the word's definition:

Deciding without knowing where it will take me,
Returning to my easel when the paints made me cry
    last week,
Dancing no matter who is watching,
Writing when there is no language to express my
    experience,
Being silent and listening,
Pursuing subjects that make me nervous,
Singing to hear my voice,
Raising my hand and saying "I will,"
Asking for dreams night after night,
Courageous is stepping off looking up not down.

Prophetic voices are often exiled in the times in which they live and then canonized in the years that follow. Look at Teilhard de Chardin, for example. For the last ten years of his life, he was permitted to publish only manuscripts that were exclusively scientific. Fortunately he had trusted friends, so, soon after his death, *The Phenomenon of Man* and *The Divine Milieu* became bestsellers. At any conference in the post-Vatican II church, these books could be seen tucked under people's arms. Teilhard's writings are the foundation stone of our current cosmological work. In his time and church, however, evolution was seen as suspect.

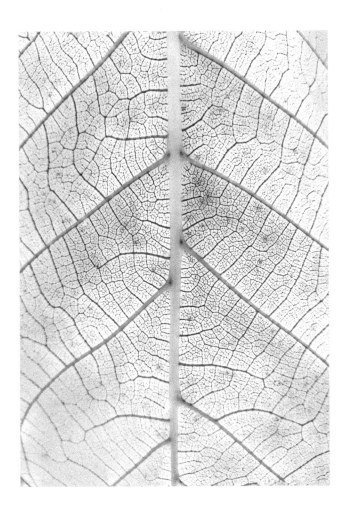

The Creative Process

The creative process is the closest we get to the divine. It is the doorway into the new story. One can't be a machine, or think like one, and be creative. The two are incompatible. The creative process is about unleashing the imagination and entering into the spirit of mysticism, which can be understood as the resurrection of our soul. It is the consciousness of a new worldview.

In our deepest self, we are at one with the universe, with ourselves, with one another, with creation, and with the divine. Standing on the corner of 4th and Walnut in downtown Louisville, Kentucky, Thomas Merton suddenly said, "I love everybody! I am awakening from the dream of separateness." *That* is what creativity does for us. It awakens us from the dream of separateness— from the nightmare of urban blight, from the despair of the youth, from the plight of old people who are put into filing cabinets called retirement communities, from the distance and alienation we feel toward the very source of our own life and being.

One of the first steps to the creative process is learning to be silent. Learning to live with silence. We can say that wisdom is the capacity for a listening heart. Through a listening heart, we are tuned in and attuned to the voice within and the voice without. Stories are based on listening and recognition. There is no story if nobody listens. There is no story if there is no one to tell it. Silence is the birthplace of creativity. It also gives us the capacity to move beyond illusion to reality. The media, on the other hand, can be a vehicle for illusion, for propaganda, or as Noam Chomsky put it, "manufactured consent." The creative process requires a movement from illusion to reality. What blocks us are our misconceptions about who we are or what it is we are called to create.

Many people have put words to this process. Gregory Baum said, "Creativity is what we believe in." In other words, faith is in the imagination. What we really believe in is what we create. Not what we claim we believe in but what we actually create reveals our deepest conviction. This is worth thinking about because often our traditions are reduced to tenets of belief rather than creative acts.

Through creativity, we confront our mortality. We experience resurrection and make it possible for the result of our creative act to live on beyond us—be it a child, a poem, a project, or an idea.

I think we should take a vow of creativity. We should vow to allow our imagination to act in ways we have not planned. The creative process is like parenting a child: first you give it life, then you give it love, and then you let it go. One of the reasons creativity is so challenging for us is that we want to control what we create. Parents know that is impossible. The same is true of a relationship. It is also true of a book or any project: you have no control over how it is understood. Creativity involves the most profound act of surrender we can engage in, allowing something to pass through us. It's a paradoxical experience because we have to be fully involved and out of the way at the same time. We need both prolonged engagement and surrender. We don't own the results of our creative acts. We don't own our imagination or what our imagination gives birth to.

Just watch Stephen Curry take a three-point shot. He is all the way out at half court, and you think he couldn't possibly make a shot from there. And then ... *swish*. Some call that *flow*. Some call that *being in the zone*. It doesn't happen only in athletics, but can appear in any part of our life: making love, making music, making stories. Being in the zone happens when we totally forget ourselves and yet remain totally conscious of the moment. That is creativity. That is self-transcendence. The theological word for this is *resurrection*. Out of death life comes, out of nothingness newness is born.

Creativity as Healing

Creativity is an instrument of healing in our lives and for the planet. Perhaps the most healing gesture we can make is to imagine that we belong. Belonging heals the deep wound of homelessness and the deep conviction that we are unhealable, eternally without a home. A friend told me that one day she awoke convinced that the capacity to imagine is at the heart of healing. I believe she was right. Creativity makes healing possible because it challenges us to visualize what our life could be like if we no longer had the physical, emotional, and spiritual limitations that keep us dis-eased.

I recall again the pear tree we had in our backyard in my hometown in Canada. I learned two things from that tree: if you pick a pear too early, it isn't any good, and if you leave it on the tree too long, it gets soft and rots. That was a lesson about creativity. There's a moment, a timing, in the creative process. Ideas need to ripen in us before they can be born. The idea of wellness needs to ripen in us before we can be healed. Creativity heals the hole in our troubled hearts; it is central to our human vocation.

The scriptures say we need to become like children again. We do that by retrieving our imagination. It is a mystical experience. It is an experience that requires both support and freedom and that results in healing for ourselves and our planet.

Wisdom and Creativity

As our traditions have retreated from relevance, spirituality has erupted in the minds and hearts of people. As faith in institutions has decreased, spirituality has increased. We have a great opportunity now. We have the opportunity to give birth to a new culture, to create not just with a paintbrush but on the "canvas" of relationships. We can create a society in which Black lives matter, women's voices are honored, Indigenous peoples are revered, traditions are revitalized, and science becomes mysticism rather than materialism. We need a new vision that will evoke positive energy, that will celebrate mystery, that will respond to the incredible hunger we have for meaning in our lives. Thus, consciousness and conscience become compatible. In a resacralized world, silence and listening will be reverenced. The prophetic voice will become our own, and we will have the creativity and the courage to express it.

At this critical point in human history, we must realize that ambiguity is probably the clearest approach we can take to describe who we are in this time of accelerated change. M.C. Richards brought this into focus for me. When asked to talk about herself, this twentieth-century poet, widely known for her book on creativity entitled *Centering*, explained that ambiguity is the best strategy to use to describe oneself. It is a way to avoid labels or stereotypes. If you label yourself by saying, "I am a doctor, or a lawyer, or a priest," you immediately become the cultural icon for that profession, with all its limits and expectations. If, however, you announce yourself with a level of ambiguity, your true self can emerge and your creative potential can be more fully realized. On a societal level, in these in-between times, we must avoid all forms of fundamentalism and the positing of absolutes where they do not exist. This is instead a time to live with messiness and to accept that from the chaos will emerge new forms that will give focus to our lives.

It is a time to ponder what the divine wants us to create. Thomas Berry calls this a moment of grace, a moment where transformation is possible, where disruption provides opportunity rather than reasons for despair. It is a time to ingest the universe story, by reading, by reflection, by ritual, and by a new kind of literacy that sees in the natural world the face of the divine. It is a time to realize that we need to let go of the world view upon which much of our society has been based. Out of this shattering of the dominant worldview, the possibility for new life will emerge.

The Twilight of the Clockwork God by J.D. Ebert is a series of interviews with six eminent scientists. The book reminds us that we live in the last days of the "clockwork god," the god who was the mechanic with the oil can and whose prized possession was Detroit, because it made machines and automobiles. It is also a time to risk being on the edge of institutions but at the center of issues. Power is no longer defined by City Hall but springs up in the neighborhoods and streets of the city, where people dare to talk about what is really important.

It is a time to face our fears—of not belonging, of rejection, of success, of suffocation, of heights, of God. To face our fear is to pave the way for a future of silence and listening. It is time for us to articulate a spirituality that will take us into tomorrow, sensitive to the pain of the planet, nourished by the beauty of creation, embraced by the divine presence in all of life. The new spirituality sees our primary impulse as one to create a better world for the offspring and the unborn of every species.

All Who Love the World

Celebrating Earth, art and spirit,
we strive to create a dynamic integration
of the ever-present now.
We bring forth the cosmic imagination
to remind us we live at the origin of things
and anticipate the future emerging in our midst.

Now is our cosmic moment, dear friend.
Welcome this day, cherish this moment.
Dissolve all separation and embrace the now.
Become the hope of yesterday,
the promise of what still needs to be done.
Allow this present moment to be here now,
all who love the world.

Liberation and Life

Gratitude and grace,
epiphanies of freedom,
speaking truth to power
transforms how it feels to be free.

Sacrament

Every word is a sacrament,
an infusion of wisdom and possibility.
Every breath an inhalation
and exhalation of existence.

Let my soul speak,
activate the overflowing beauty
of this sacred moment.

Listen to the pulse of the planet,
embrace the soul of the cosmos,
as each new moment punctuates
the heartbeat of the universe.

Wisdom Sources

If we are to live in a healthy relationship with the universe, we need to heed and honor four sources of wisdom—women, Indigenous peoples, classical traditions, and science—that are repressed in our society. We don't hear women's voices the way we should. Indigenous peoples have been abused. The classical traditions have retreated from relevance. And science has become materialism. But there is something to retrieve in all these wisdom sources.

We need to draw forth the voices that are not heard and celebrated. These voices are revelatory. They have been oppressed but they are most authentically the voice of the divine.

The sense of inclusivity is one central contribution of women's wisdom that is absolutely counter to the patriarchal culture of hierarchical dualism. Body is connected to mind, Earth to person. Women's wisdom nurtures a dialectical and inclusive consciousness on all levels.

Indigenous peoples express an integral presence to the community of life. The postindustrial society does not. One of the reasons we honor Indigenous peoples is that they remind us that we are embedded in the dynamics of life, that each of us carries indigenous wisdom in our own soul, even if it is deeply hidden.

To be totally free, we need to come to terms with our roots of our classical traditions. We can't just say, "That's not going to work." We're culturally coded into these traditions, and they have much more influence on us than we think. We need to retrieve the best of these traditions, particularly their mystical and prophetic dimensions, and reflect on them in the context of the universe itself.

Science reveals much about our spiritual journey. Through reflecting on evolution, we discover that the great transformational moments of the universe have parallels in our lives. The flaring forth of the original fireball reminds us of our own beginnings and the events that have taken place over time. The formation of Earth invites us to ponder our connection to creation and the beauty that is ours to commune with. The bursting forth of life on Earth, the plants and animals, reminds us that we are deeply related to all the members of the Earth community.

The birth of the human challenges each of us to assume our responsibility as a people to live in a more mutually enhancing way with Earth and every species.

By integrating into our lives the characteristics of the bioregion, the wisdom of women and of Indigenous peoples, the mystical and prophetic roots of our traditions, and the scientific principles of the universe, we can deepen our relationship with creation and live with planet Earth in a more mutually enhancing way.

Contemplation and Life: Action/Reflection

What encounters with people and with nature have deepened your desire to ponder the meaning of freedom and existence?

What holds you back from being fully present and engaging in a life of freedom and fulfillment for every species?

How have these moments of intimacy nurtured your efforts to be an instrument of liberation for people and the planet?

In what way has creativity deepened your capacity in the art of life?

To plumb the mysterious depths of life we must:

- Plunge into the deepest recesses of the human heart and the heart of the universe
- Play, pray, act, reflect, write, create, relate, dialogue, remain silent, and become newly aware of and connected to the person we can become, and more fully realize the deeper purpose of our existence and calling
- Become fully immersed in and critically aware of our toxic culture, yet not obsessed by it, so we can learn to create clarity in our imagination and focus in our heart as we strive to "become delivered to our self" and transform toxicity into justice
- Surrender to the wild energy of the cosmos, whose power and potential take us to a new level of uncertainty and surprise, where the universe, activated by the divine creative energy, can do its work and we can do ours

- Relax, don't "force the river" while creating the capacity to become fully focused and engaged, yet detached from the outcome
- Be willing to ponder the possibility that the universe can become our teacher and the template for a new vision of engagement and justice that can transcend and surpass previous approaches, which were too often embedded in formats of domination and inversion rather than conversion, power over rather than power from within, division rather than inclusion

Part 3
Longing of Earth

Canticle to Earth

An engaged spirituality that takes us to the edge of our longing for Earth includes the following:

We can read the signs of the times in our toxic culture, without becoming unduly obsessive so that our clarity is clouded and our hope in danger of despair.

We achieve the exquisite balance between an activism whose overemphasis moves us away from our center and a verbalism that, when out of balance, diminishes our engagement in the transformation of the world.

We discover, relate to, and collaborate with people and projects whose worldviews and commitments are aligned with our own.

We commit to nurturing a culture of hope and a healthy creation, and in so doing, dispel the tendencies toward despair and demonization that are rampant in our dominant culture.

We provide access to fresh energy and a zest for life by engaging in an unmediated mysticism through which we experience oneness with self, life, creation, and the divine.

We dissolve tendencies toward arrogance or isolation by nurturing the commonalities with our worldviews, our traditions, and our commitment to creation through our actions in the world.

We hold periodic gatherings where we come together to break bread and tell stories, creating opportunities for practices and partnerships of transformation that are innovative and aligned to our new and emerging worldview.

We create a balanced dynamic between tradition (continuity) and innovation (discontinuity) that ventures to the frontiers of reflection as we move beyond theology to an operative cosmology.

Longing of Creation

Beyond the longing of soul and life resides a deeper hunger, a longing of Earth. A longing of every species to commune, interact, and be admired. The longing of Earth is engaged in through the revelatory moments that happen when we experience Earth through our senses. In sight, sound, touch, and smell, we listen to the language and longings of creation.

Each species, with its particular gifts and desire to interact, invites admiration. At the very heart of each being resides the essence of its existence and the capacity to relate. The very Earth desires to commune with its individuated self—be that animal, vegetable, or mineral.

The reflections here are predicated on the conviction that Earth is a seamless garment that encompasses both the social and ecological dimensions of life.

The Oblate Ecological Initiative

The Oblate Ecological Initiative, based in Illinois, has been running Earth literacy, restoration projects, and other ecological initiatives for many years. When I visited, we assembled in a room with spacious windows overlooking the Mississippi River. The voice of Darrell filled the room. He was a man of seasoned years and profound commitment. He spoke of acts of justice and citizen diplomacy that were both frightening and inspiring to hear, such as a story of working among the poor in Brazil with Dom Helder Camara. His narrative touched only briefly upon the highlights of his prophetic journey, and I felt moved to ask, "As a man so committed to a life of justice, how do you view the project of an ecological learning center in relation to all that you have done and the issues that have captured your energy and your life?" Without hesitation he declared decisively, 'This is by far the most important."

Later, as we walked around the grounds and visited the newly planted organic garden, I acknowledged that the work of ecology and Earth-based spirituality is a defining task for our generation. I realized at a new level that the work of Earth literacy is truly a work of justice.

Earth literacy is an adventure in reviving the ancient language of creation spoken by all life, a language we have disregarded in favor of that spoken only by humans. Creation itself, not any religion's scripture, is the primary vehicle of communication between the divine and humanity. Within this garden, I became aware that the process of cultivating, growing, harvesting, consuming, and planting is a profound experience, not just for maintaining our health but for attuning our lives to the dynamics of the universe and the processes of Earth.

Later, as I contemplated the events of our day, I remembered and celebrated parallel projects taking place in different parts of the United States as well as in Ireland, Australia, New Zealand, Africa, Korea, and Canada. Suddenly they seemed like lights illuminating the darkness of our cultural soul.

Silence of the Woods

Listen to the silence,
to the magic in the woods.
Follow the call,
be guided by the stars.
Reweave the tapestry of your life,
become alive again.
Let this threshold moment
unleash what's next
as you listen
to the silence of the woods.

A Hymn to Creation

Poetry invites us to know again the place
where finitude and infinity meet,
where words of mystery envelop
the landscape that lies deep within.

Poetry washes over us
as words, however lyrical,
announce once more that they are
the last resort for what lies deep within.

The new story unfurls before us,
unleashing the divine imagination,
announcing the cosmological powers
that swirl through the universe
and become proclaimed with fresh comprehension
of humanity's conscious self-awareness.

Peace making brings *cosmos* back to Earth.
With renewed hope, we feel again
the possibility of a beloved community.
A place where peace can happen always,
where hope becomes our oxygen,
a source of breath.

Where we can once again inspire each other
and aspire to a healed and healthy Earth,
a place of energy and zest
where we can become instruments of promise,
a people of planetary peace.

A people who know
that the universe is
constitutive to all our traditions
and a sacred experience for openness and life.

Realizing the Dream

Maurice Lange, founder of the Oblate Ecological Initiative, told the story of realizing his dream of an ecological learning center and community-supported agriculture project. In so doing, he described the elements of a dream. These guidelines are helpful as we develop the direction and purpose of our own visionary existence.

The elements for realizing the dream were as follows:

Pay attention. Retrieve dreams from your childhood that awakened a passion for life and that remain with you today. Perhaps a relative introduced you to the beauty of the natural world.

Honor intuition. Trust the deeper visceral knowing that is revealed when you focus on the wisdom that is available when you pay attention to sacred impulses and inner promptings.

Let the dream evolve. Let the deep desire, the longing, change and evolve. Dreams are guided more by a compass than a map. Allow the deep longing to change the direction of your life rather than becoming fixated on a predetermined goal.

Broaden your learning. Your dream will change when you widen the context and see the universe as the container for your journey. Understand your dream as an expression of the dream of Earth.

Live the dream. Your dream will require a practice. Be true to your deepest desire and make your actions as congruent as possible with the vision of how your life can be.

Find good companions on the way. To persevere and realize your dream requires that you have good companions on the way, fellow travelers with whom you can dream and act together. Offer and receive support as you journey forth in the realization of your dream.

Stay in it for the long haul. To realize your dream requires prolonged engagement, the willingness to have a vision, passion, and the willingness to work.

Earthaven Ecovillage

Earthaven Ecovillage is nestled in the mountains of North Carolina, just outside the city of Asheville. Within this unassuming yet daring experiment, I saw glimpses of the world that our deepest longing calls us to build. From the time I first heard of it in 1995, I felt called to visit this experiment in living within the dynamics of Earth.

At Earthaven, men, women, and children discover new ways to build homes, to access power, and to gain a livelihood. They are totally off the commercial electric grid. Their energy is solar, they grow their own food, they build their own homes. This shared activity affords them a space for both privacy and relationship, contemplation and intimacy. Earthaven is an intergenerational community whose goal is to live in a mutually enhancing manner with the land. Through courage, imagination, and commitment, they dedicate their labor to sustainability.

One Sunday evening, I joined them in their community center, a thirteen-sided building whose architecture reflects the Mayan solar calendar. There I met people who had followed their dreams to participate in this potential prototype for the future of our race. They have made a radical break with the consumerism of the dominant American culture and live a life of simplicity in order to build a better world for their children, where lifestyle does not come at the price of pollution or depletion of Earth's finite resources. Following the introductions, we began our dialogue by relating the story of the universe and its transformations from the initial fireball to the galactic, Earth, life, and human periods in order to create a context in which to place the personal narratives of Earthaven and its creators. The responses were powerful, spontaneous, and moving.

One of the members told of the original formulation of the dream, the shattering of previous attempts, and how the group had finally secured the property on which Earthaven is being built. Subsequently, others chimed in about how they came to join this adventure and what brought them to this sacred place, now a beacon of hope and a growing manifestation of the "reinvention of humanity and culture" of which Thomas Berry so eloquently speaks.

As we listened to the stories of how people felt called to Earthaven, it seemed to me they were cultural canaries driven from the toxicity of the outside world to form a sustainable community. One man told of riding his bicycle across the country to take a course in permaculture, only to remain and raise a family. Some spoke of searching for a way of life apart from the consumption-mad world. Others recounted their disenchantment with corporate America, and their deep desire to live intentionally. Some of the older people announced that having raised their families, they were free to live in the manner they had always wished. As the stories continued, they were punctuated by laughter, spontaneous revelations, and moments of clarity. One could feel that the community center was a place where the pathologies of pollution and social disintegration could be healed through the birth of a new vision.

I saw Earthaven as a laboratory for deep cultural therapy. With arduous effort and great hope, people are fashioning an ecovillage, a new way of living. They are literally beginning again, moving forward with new insights. With a sensitivity to Earth, a new vision of lifestyle and livelihood emerges. They generate electricity with solar panels and build straw-bale homes. Through biodynamic gardening, they grow their own food. The methods employed in each of these activities manifest a new way to live with health and wholeness on Earth.

We had begun the evening by coming together in a circle and singing the chant "If we're here for anything at all, it's to take care of Earth!" As we dispersed at the end of the evening, the chant reverberated in my ears, and I felt very connected to this noble experiment that challenges us to dream new dreams, imagine new lives.

Imagining Newness

Energy flows like molten lava
as the imagination erupts,
and from this place of birth and possibility,
a new creation is born.
As we begin to pulsate with all that's possible,
our world continues to unfold,
and much that is new shows up.
Let there be light in the darkness,
peace in war, sunshine at dawn,
wonder in day and reverence at dusk,
returning to an enduring peace.

Meant to Be

You only possess what you give away—
your imagination, your heart,
your dreams, your beauty,
and all for which you hope.
Now is the time to reinvent yourself,
to wonder about your soul,
about who you are and who you can be.
Listen to the promptings of Earth
and discover what you can give away.
This is how to become who you are meant to be!

A Second Superpower for Planetary Peace

As Dante needed Virgil in order to descend into the Inferno and return liberated and free, we as a people require the strength and healing properties of a new religious/spiritual sensitivity to confront the destructiveness in our midst and emerge as the people of a planetary peace.

Through deepening our spirituality, we can restore a withering and destructive culture and gain access to the psychic energy necessary to take our place as peacemakers in today's.

Twenty years ago, *New York Times* journalist Patrick Tyler coined the term *second superpower* to refer to world public opinion as a force for peace. Although that second superpower did not succeed at the time in stopping the Iraq war, as it hoped to do, it did begin to build the large force of Internet-based activism.

Since then, we have witnessed numerous global protests. In 2020, protests following the murder of George Floyd spread to Europe, South America, and Asia, as people around the world resonated with their own experiences of colonialism, racism, and state violence. Similarly, the March for Our Lives movement, while instigated to stop the uniquely American problem of gun violence, saw support protests in many countries around the world.

As part of the Global Climate Strike, growing out of the protests by activist Greta Thunberg, young people marched in one hundred fifty countries in 2019. Their efforts continue through the Fridays for Future movement and other climate activism.

Notably, these movements are led by young people, who understand that their very future depends on their willingness to stand up for a world without violence and war, a world without colonialism and racial oppression, a world that takes action on climate, a world in which all can live in peace.

This peace will be:

- More than a truce; it will be lasting peace based in love and forgiveness
- Recognition that the life of a child is more important than anyone's right to bear arms
- A yes to reverence, dialogue, and sensitivity, as well as to economic and educational security and affordable housing security
- A no to violence, poverty, ignorance, homelessness, racism, imperialism, and ecological devastation
- A yes to mercy, kindness, cooperation, and a convergence of the heart, whereby we summon the courage to stand up for freedom, take back our country, heal all separation, celebrate the sheer joy of living, and realize there will be no peace on Earth until there is peace with Earth

Together we can forge:

- A culture of confidence and depth
- A culture of compassion and admiration
- A culture of beauty and identity for each participant
- A culture of concern and reciprocity
- A culture of creativity and engagement

- A culture of gratitude and collaboration
- A culture of struggle and fulfillment
- A culture of challenge and change
- A culture of action and reflection
- A culture of story and deep listening
- A culture of justice and reverence for the voiceless
- A culture of flexibility and focus
- A culture of transcendence and transformation
- A culture of tenderness and strength
- A culture of intimacy and contemplation
- A culture of amazement and mutuality
- A culture of listening and recognition
- A culture of mysticism and engagement

Five Stations of Hope

One evening when I taught at the Sophia Center in Holy Names University, I wrote a question on the board: "What is your vision of a dynamic relationship between the new story and the culture?" In other words, how can we contribute to the creation of a new culture based on our understanding of the new cosmology?

The students created a ritual that was a profound response to the question. First, we were invited to proceed through an arch symbolizing a rite of passage into a context for a new consciousness and a new culture, a place of geo-justice and engaged cosmology.

Once in this new space, we were invited to visit each of five stations at our own pace. Although they were offered to us in no particular order, I felt there was an intrinsic logic to the process.

I visited the Earth station first. There, we were invited to plant a seed in the moist soil provided and to water it. We then placed a paper cup containing the newly planted seed among the candles that illuminated the darkness of the room. This station I named the vocation station, the place where the seeds of our passion for Earth can grow and flourish.

Next I moved to the wishing-well station. There, we were invited to take a pebble from a tray and place it in a wishing well while making a wish for Earth. My wish was that everyone present would be able to live in such a way that our wishes for Earth could be realized. In turn I named this station "the vision station," feeling deeply that if our vocations and the call of Earth were to be realized, if our seeds were to grow, they would need to be supported and fostered by a vision strong and clear enough to make that possible.

From the wishing well, I moved to the meditation station. There, people were sitting on cushions or chairs, surrounded by quotations such as "Mysticism is the number one anchor for global solidarity" (David Steindl-Rast). As I joined the others at this station, it became profoundly clear, once again, that a new, creative, and just culture will only be realized when we who are committed to the task recognize that deep, consistent spiritual practices, such as sitting in meditation, will be necessary. Only then will our vocations flourish and our dreams bear fruit.

Next I was drawn to the poetry station. There, we were invited to compose a poem and place it on a multi-colored banner. I wrote:

Cosmic origins
Reveal the source of life
From which beauty flows.

As we responded to the invitation to create, I realized, as if for the first time, how significant the imagination is on the journey to justice making. The culture that awaits us has no predetermined patterns or outcomes. If we are to realize our vocations and our visions, and continue our spiritual practices, it will always be necessary to liberate the imagination in order to create a culture of justice and peace.

At the final station, the action station, I began to sign a petition to preserve our fragile planet and to write postcards to political leaders seeking their support. In doing so, I realized that an engaged spirituality culminating in action is an essential component of the process of bringing about a dynamic relationship between our culture and our cosmology.

As the evening concluded, we were asked to gather in a large circle in the center. This mandala, or symbolic image of the cosmos and Earth, also represented each of us. We placed our seeds, pebbles, prayers, poems, petitions, and postcards in the mandala and created a community based on geo-justice and engaged cosmology. Each of us was present in the mandala, including the stations we had visited. As we savored the energy present in the room, I felt more positive about the future and grateful to be among this dedicated and creative community of learners. I was grateful for the five stations of hope.

Always Nurturing

With gratitude for
the freshness of the air,
the wisdom of the trees,
the hunger of the soul,
and acceptance of the divine,
always inclusive and nurturing new life.

Easter Again

The sun peeks out
and rises in the East
as the ocean becomes the empty tomb
from which our Easter flows.
Alleluias ripple on the beach
as huddled pilgrims meet the morning
and celebrate a breath of newness
that resonates across the Eastern sky.
It's Easter again,
resurrection happens,
hope has transcended all despair,
and we are, once again, radically alive.

Bioregions: A Compass for the Journey

I have found it helpful to use the concept of bioregions to draw out the implications of our relationship with life and with all creation. A bioregion is a self-contained dimension of Earth, defined by ecological boundaries such as waterways, trees, and hill lines. It is defined not by human political systems but by Earth itself. For example, I was born in the Great Lakes bioregion on the St. Clair River, which unites Lake Huron and Lake St. Clair.

A Context for Life

A bioregion is a complex structure made up of differentiated but mutually supportive life systems that are self-sustaining. Some characteristics of a bioregion are especially relevant to our understanding of how we are to relate to one another and to our environment.

A Context for Self-Propagation

The first such characteristic is self-propagation. If a bioregion is going to be healthy, every species has to have space to sustain life, to build its house, so to speak. The same thing applies for the human community: we need enough space to surround us, and so we have room for both intimacy and contemplation. Living with others doesn't mean we don't need and want privacy. Living alone doesn't mean that we don't need and want community. To receive what we need and long for, we must understand the needs and wants of the creatures with whom we share the space, and we must negotiate so that nothing and no one is left out.

A Context for Reciprocity

A bioregion is also self-nourishing. One of the great examples of the self-nourishing universe is the relationship between a mammal and a tree. A mammal exhales carbon dioxide and inhales oxygen, while a tree takes in carbon dioxide and gives off oxygen. That's why such a great climate disaster is created when we cut down the rainforest: our very ability to breathe is compromised.

In the human community, we also need balance. For example, there should be balance between introverts and extroverts; some people can go off on their own for the day, while others can seek company. We need to respect our differences but also realize that a certain amount of reciprocity is required.

Reciprocity is the human mode of the universe's capacity for self-nourishment. For example, when we say, "I'll cultivate the potatoes, because than I'll have food for the winter," both plants and humans thrive. In this way entropy, the loss of energy within the system, is minimized.

A Context for Guidance

The third important characteristic of a bioregion is that it is self-educating. Some decades ago, people interested in growing spiritually had spiritual directors. That spiritual director sometimes was thought to be the voice of God telling you what to do. I think the universe itself is our best spiritual director; we can engage in its rhythms in ways that evoke and create responses in ourselves.

Our pets can be our spiritual directors. If you have a cat, the cat knows exactly what's going on with you. They come up to you if you're sad and leave you alone if you're angry. Pets are like that. So is the whole universe.

We can learn so much from living interdependently with all of life, while not reducing our spiritual journey's guidance to a human sitting in a chair across the room from us. Having a spiritual director can be useful at time; it's another mirror, but it's not the only one. For some, it's not the most liberating. To sit under a tree and write poetry could be a wonderful exercise in spiritual guidance. So could paying attention to our dreams and other ways of gaining access to our inmost selves and the divine creative energy in our lives.

A Context for Freedom

Fourth, bioregions are self-governing. One way to understand this is to realize that nobody holds absolute power. Often humans interpret self-governing to mean "Nobody knows what they're doing around here" or "The place seems disorganized." And then they immediately want to step in and exercise authority to get things under control. There is much to be learned, however, if instead of jumping in to make things run as we think they should, we step back and ask to be shown what is the most creative way to participate in the life of the whole.

This may be uncomfortable because, when we step outside an oppressive structure, our own internalized oppression may become evident. However, when we no longer buy into that system, it is easier to free ourselves from what holds us back at a personal level. Then our internal structure gets stronger. At that point, liberation can take place.

A Context for Healing

This leads us into another dimension of bioregions: they are self-healing. The medical and psychological professions tend to operate by seeking to remove the parts of us deemed unhealthy rather than by returning us to a harmonious relationship with the whole. If you look at how your body works, how Earth works, however, you will see that it is self-healing. If you cut yourself, the body heals itself. This is equally true of the soul and psyche. What we need is to stimulate the psyche so that healing can take place. This does not necessarily involve analysis or getting and giving advice. It can be simply about getting the energy moving in your soul, in your psyche, in your total person, so the woundedness you feel will heal as naturally as a cut finger.

We need to be sensitive to each other so healing can be maximized for everyone. We need to both respect each person's journey and challenge each other in loving ways. We need to respect and support this same self-healing in the plants, animals, minerals, and bacteria with which we share this planet so that a truly healthy ecosystem can emerge as a home for all of us.

A Context for Purpose

Bioregions are self-emerging. Materialist science says the universe is not going anywhere, it has no real intention or real purpose, and life is meaningless. A bioregional model, however, says there is an innate purpose to our lives, to a particular region of Earth, and to our own journey. We are here to help each other discover our life purpose, our passion, and what really engages us, so we can do it as fully as possible, and can also give our gift to others. Usually life changes happen when we awaken to the unexpected. Spirituality is about being attentive to the unexpected and responsive to it; it is about aligning our energies with the unfolding dynamics of the universe.

When we integrate these characteristics of bioregions into our lives—by self-propagating, self-nourishing, self-educating, self-healing, and self-emerging—we have responded to a deep longing to experience this planet as our home.

Celebrate

Pay homage to origins,
honor the cosmic womb,
be grateful for beauty,
remember your story.

Pay attention to this moment,
listen to your heart,
rediscover hope,
Become what you were meant to be.

Embrace the crucible,
welcome the primordial furnace,
notice moments of the unexpected.
Each an opportunity to celebrate.

Within this arch of wisdom,
relationships extend
energizing commitment to a hope-filled life,
transcending all despair.

Reflection at the Edge of Earth

Mary Whelan, an Irish author, community development worker, and founder of the Community Action Network in Dublin, declared that the basic characteristic needed in an activist for change is the cultivation of gratitude and grace. Gratitude is the capacity for heartfelt appreciation. Grateful people know in their hearts that what they have received is a gift. In fact, they approach life—whether the dawning of a new day, the love of a partner, the beauty of a lake or meadow, or the wonder of the imagination—with gratitude. For grateful people, partnerships and reciprocity are works of the heart. Modern community development is too often a mechanical process in which no one invests their heart. That can only produce a community lacking soul.

Mary and her colleagues worked to "ensoul" community development. This included an extended ritual on the four paths of creation/spirituality (awe, letting go, creativity, and transformation). Through their efforts, soul work found a home in community development. City planners and the citizens they sought to house benefited from a shared inner journey and began to work together as partners.

As I sat in the kitchen at the Community Action Network's office, a woman spoke for all of us when she said, "Our challenge is to integrate all of this—that is to say, the cosmology and the call to justice." She named the need to heal the separateness between the spirit and the street, vision and despair, ritual and rigidity, the wounded heart and a planet both beautiful and in pain. I saw the Community Action Network as a womb for what many of us had been longing for—a context where cosmology comes home to the street, where intuition and cognition meet, where justice and equality are extended to both people in poverty and the impoverished Earth.

The Community Action Network continues its work decades later, using their model for change, which comprises four steps:

Breaking the silence. The lived experience of those affected by social injustice or inequality is named and identified.

Inside out analysis. The systems, structures, and processes that cause and perpetuate inequality are questioned and explained from the lived perspective of those affected.

Imagining a better future. Strong community leadership imagines and creates a vision for building new structures that change in action.

Moving together. Collective action for change depends on developing sustainable cross-issue partnerships.

The Shimmering Well by the Sea

I composed this poem in honor of Mary Whalen in County Mayo, Ireland, where I visited her and saw her and her colleagues gathering to do soul work.

More than a collection of lumber and stone,
more than a place to live,
more than a hearth and a symbol of home
is the shimmering well by the sea.

More than a beautiful building now in place,
more than a dream now come true,
more than a context to gather and talk
is the shimmering well by the sea.

More than a home for the restless heart,
more than a project for peace,
more than haven to heal the soul
is the shimmering well by the sea.

More than a place to be equal and just,
more than a place to be free,
more than a place for the integral life
is the shimmering well by the sea.

More than a place to listen and learn,
more than a place to just be,
more than a place for beauty and balance
is the shimmering well by the sea.

Yes it's a place for stories and dreams,
a place of mystery for me,
as we build for Earth souls of justice and peace
at the shimmering well by the sea.

The Call to Justice Making

There are two ways we are drawn into the work of justice.

The first is as the wounded healer, like one alcoholic staying sober by helping another alcoholic to sober up. When we are dislocated from our own pain, our own woundedness, we are empowered to heal others based on our own incompleteness.

We also are drawn into justice by the deep joy that draws us passionately forward into our lives. It is our vocational destiny, our place in the great work of life, our generational task, our historical mission. We work for justice because we feel called in our souls to do so.

Against the Grain

We remember
and make present
the little ones of God.
In our recollection,
we proclaim
that poverty is not their destiny.
The denial of significance is.
A condition of injustice,
a doorway to death,
a challenge to courageously
go against the grain.
The past becomes present,
life is transformed.
We criticize the moment,
engage in creative action,
celebrate beauty,
experience hope,
are healed in our longing
for unconditioned love.

Cosmology and Our Traditions

We are in an in-between time. Thomas Aquinas took the Aristotelian cosmology and developed through his theology a reinterpretation, a re-languaging if you will, of the Christian message through the Aristotelian cosmology. We are now in a different cosmological era, but we haven't completed the theological reflection necessary to fully integrate these insights into our tradition.

Like people on a trapeze, we have let go of one rope and hover over the net, waiting for the next rope to appear.

I think the Christian story is even stronger in this new perspective. The new story brings fresh energy and a zest for life that couldn't be achieved with the old categories because they are burdened with a cosmology that has gotten us into trouble—not just ecclesiastically but industrially, educationally, and politically.

I welcome the task.

I believe in the gospel of life, that touches every aspect of our lives.

I believe that the divine presence permeates every moment.

I believe that all life is sacred.

I believe that we are summoned by the gospel to a life of peace, prayer, compassion, and justice making.

I believe the call to work for transformation is a special gift.

I think we're in the beginning of a meta-religious movement that we will cocreate together, a movement that is emerging from the consciousness of the new cosmology. The forms of religious life, of parishes, of families can be reinvented in a holistic and just way.

I don't have the answer as to what the changes will look like, but I resonate with the question. I truly feel the gospel was written in a book in words, but there is a primary revelation of divine communication that takes place through creation.

As Thomas Aquinas said, we have two scriptures to read: the book of the Bible and the book of the natural world. We need to be exegetes of both—to understand what Isaiah says, what John says, what Matthew says, but also to understand the birds, the flowers, the plants, your children, your students, and the people you work with, because they are divine revelatory sources as well. I think we need to be called back to learn that language.

The Sixth Extinction Spasm

In the final weeks of World War II, America dropped the atomic bomb on Japan. Loss of life was catastrophic. People awakened to a stark reality: if life was to continue on our Earth home, it would be necessary for nations to arrive at an agreement to disengage from nuclear warfare.

This defining moment led to the emergence of the Cold War. Since then, there have been precarious moments when the unleashing of a nuclear bomb seemed imminent—perhaps none more terrifying than resulting from Russia's invasion of Ukraine. Now, in addition to the threat of a hot nuclear war, we have the lethal threat of ecological devastation.

Scientists speak of tipping points in climate change, beyond which the damage is considered irreversible and inexorable. These tipping points include the melting of Greenland's ice sheet, the die-back of the Amazon rain forest, the collapse of currents in the Atlantic ocean, the die-off of coral reefs. There is no single tipping point, and one tipping point can trigger multiple other tipping points. Perhaps the most significant news about tipping points is that they are being reached much more rapidly than scientists previously thought. The sea level rise and temperature increases that are being set in motion now will affect generations for centuries to come.

One effect of the damage already done is what scientists recognize as the sixth mass extinction event, which is now well underway. Some have predicted that anywhere from one quarter to one half of all species will be extinct by the end of this century.

The diminishment of natural beauty—not to mention vital resources—has prompted some to say that species loss is like tearing a page from sacred scripture. For those of us who embrace a theological view—that creation is a book of primary revelation, that God is in all things, and all things are in God—the reality of species extinction leads us to a painful conclusion: it is possible to have death without a resurrection.

Song for a New Creation

Where there are ruptures in creation,
we are aroused to peace.
Where there is disquietude,
we are invited to balance.
Where there is discord,
we are attuned to resonance.
In and through the pain of our wounded planet,
we are called to make our Easter with Earth.
From collapse and devastation,
we rediscover within the risen heart of the universe.

A Blessing

Blessed is Earth:
it shall flourish with radiant beauty.
Blessed are the waters:
they will flow with clarity and quench our thirst.
Blessed are the trees:
they shall absorb toxins and give us breath.
Blessed are the birds:
they shall soar stately in the sky.
Blessed are those in pain:
they shall discover radiance in the dark.
Blessed are those who despair:
they shall be enveloped in hopeful peace.
Blessed is the fire:
it shall melt all walls and separation
with the energies of love.
Blessed are they who live in the universe,
and celebrate the resacralization of the planet:
they shall experience beauty in all that *is* revealed.

Autocosmology: Our Continuing Quest

What is an appropriate expression of our experience of the cosmos and our personal interactions in the world?

We search for a fresh formation of consciousness, an awareness that will deconstruct past practices and evoke fresh approaches in our quest for life. We become aware that the human mind is deepening and forming a new consciousness. This awareness will shape and form an emerging vision and a fresh sense of our destiny as an unfolding expression of what it means to be human.

We are increasingly aware that we are irresistibly engaged in witnessing humanity's enhanced capacity to respond to the dynamics of a time-developmental consciousness. This enhanced awareness takes us to the precipice of new beginnings, a context where we can reinvent ourselves and our understanding of the universe.

When we awake in the morning, we can proclaim with confidence "this is who I am." We are the original flaring forth, the primordial fireball.

Words fail to grasp and express what is happening. We move from a consciousness of resources to one of relationship.

Our task then is to incarnate creativity expressed in and through the dream of Earth and the cosmos, to engage in the transformation of culture and the institutions of the world. With something more significant to live for, we move forward to reinvent society, our consciousness, and the soul of the planet.

Prayer for Cosmogenesis

May I plunge into an ocean of grace,
dissolve all memories of a world divided,
of soul work that remains static and stuck.
Today we are invited to plunge into a world of oneness,
to become the sacred soul we are meant to be.
Now is the time to become our true self.
Enjoy the discovery,
awake to this moment,
celebrate a fresh awareness of this expanding universe.

The Way Ahead

As we look to the future with hope and envision the deepest fulfillment of the longing present in creation, we see a sense of place to gather, imagine, heal, commune, receive, and extend hospitality, to reverence diversities of cultures and traditions, to enhance consciousness, increase awareness, and honor Earth. Here there is a place for children, a context for learning and Earth literacy, for nurturing an evolving consciousness experienced in a kinesthetic way. Relationships are grounded in friendship and shared paths of service and compassion.

This emerging process may be described in many ways, such as a garden, a web, or a constellation. As a garden, each person or project is a flower, a unique expression of beauty and compassion, rooted in our common Earth. As a web, it is neither vertical nor horizontal, but nonhierarchical, transparent at the center, and strong on the edges. As a constellation, it is part of the new cosmology and multi-centric, with every participating person and project residing at the center of an emerging constellation of relationships. In each case, there is a home for those participating in an engaged cosmology, a place where they can find rest, refreshment, and renewal.

In this emerging context, the vision is characterized by networks of information, support, and common action, acts of hospitality, and catalytic interactions that nurture experimentation, prophetic acts, deep wisdom, reciprocity, mutuality and the experience of belonging. Each project and person will receive support for their issue, passion, or call.

I envision a council of all beings, where humans stand in the center and all the other species have a chance to talk to the humans about how they have mistreated the land: "I don't like what you're doing to my water" or "Why did you cut down my trees?" Then the humans come to the outside and apologize to all the other species, who are now in the center. This council of all species would be what Thomas Berry called an "Eozoic council." It would support and energize prophetic groups that are springing up all over the country and all over the world. We need to lend our voices to making the planet a mutually enriching place to live, not just for us but for the children of the next generation and beyond.

The council will understand itself as a cosmic circle, open to fresh energy, the evolving nature of human consciousness, and our collective call to participate in the great work. The ethos of the Ecozoic council is one of openness and deep listening. The Ecozoic council's mission is to:

- Nurture and support a planetary consciousness, a cosmology that focuses on actions that are global, local, and personal
- Support the ecologically affirming initiatives of globalization in regard to human rights and environmental work
- Promote circles of shared wisdom, information, support, and common action, whereby people and projects become aware of their unique contributions to the great work and provide willing support for those engaged in diverse efforts

- Provide the opportunity and context, whereby participants in the council and their colleagues are able to reflect on and articulate an operative cosmology that will ground them in their personal journey, culture, and tradition and the cosmos as they strive to engage in their contribution to the historical mission of humanity at this time

Through listening deeply to each other and learning of the work to which we are called, members of the council will have the opportunity to see the uniqueness of their efforts and achieve an increased appreciation for the diverse yet global nature of our common task.

Through interaction and shared resources, participants will grow in the capacity to clarify and focus their strategies and action plans from each of the programs and projects presented to the council.

Through dialogue and critical reflection, participants will become collectively aware of the issues around which they share a common commitment and that can serve as a focus for a common action to energize and focus the council and the constituent groups they represent.

The Ecozoic council will provide an opportunity to raise our spirituality, cosmology, and consciousness to a new level and contribute to mutual enhancement through the interaction with every species in and through Earth, while fulfilling the collective goal of preparing a better world for the children of every species.

Many years ago, Archimedes said, "Give me a lever long enough and a fulcrum on which to place it, and I shall move the world." It is my hope that through the experience of sacredness and depth and the practice of

162

engaged cosmology, we may in some small way make our contribution to the world for which we long.

The Search

Diving deep into the cosmic water of uncertainty,
new frontiers of exploration beckon
without answers or focused invitation.
Magnetic intuition draws me forth
into a gravitational adventure of the soul.
Newfound engagement stirs deeply;
in the uncertainty of the moment, a shattering occurs.
As once, as if forever and yet for the first time,
a cosmic vista emerges and unfolds.
Incarnation happens at the epicenter of my soul
as I begin to understand at least for now and maybe later
that I am a child of the universe,
a child longing for wisdom and searching for home.
Longing to discover relatedness
and the deep nurturing mystery
that is the resource for connectedness
and the resonating fire of my soul,
I wander in search of meaning, purpose, passion, and life.
Wander forth in search of wonder and surprise.
Wander forth in search of balance, wisdom, and a
    listening heart.
Wander forth in search of my place in an unfolding
    universe
Wander forth in search of a newfound strength
to struggle and discover within the recesses of my soul
the wellspring I dare to call my life.
Wander forth in careless abandon,
always giving notice that my place in the universe
is contained in the seeds of all that I am, have been, and
    will become.

All that has led up to this galactic moment of wisdom and
    surprise,
has cascaded into consciousness and culminated in the
    person that is me.
Those geological events formed our planet home
and now are the basis of our being.
Those incidents of new life sprang forth from the sea
and flourish now on the hillside of our home.
Those momentous moments of fresh understanding
have become this gorgeous planet,
now newly conscious of celebrating itself.
And so the journey continues,
wrapped in an envelope of uncertainty,
embracing both hope and terror.
With a newfound vision of tomorrow
and a peace that may never cease.

Contemplation and Earth: Action/Reflection

What experiences of the other-than-human world have shaped your senses of the sacred and influenced the trajectory of your life?

How have the rhythms of each day, of the seasons—with the anticipation of spring, the abundance of summer, the vulnerable beauty of autumn, and the waiting of winter—animated your soul?

How has your relationship with the natural world awakened in you a desire to care for Earth?

In what ways do you feel called to respond to the devastation of Earth and resacralize creation?

How do you feel moved to respond with courage and respect to the promise and possibility present in each expression of creation?

We must become planetary citizens of harmony, balance, and peace. People whose imaginations perceive a world of geo-justice and who hope for a better world for the children of every species. People who perceive the new cosmology as a studio for personal, cultural, and ecological transformation and a research arena for discovering practices and approaches to a mystical and engaged cosmology that:

- Is congruent with the new cosmology
- Is aligned to a more mutually enhancing future
- Is deeply connected to the trajectory of our own story
- Finds expression and culminates in a culture of compassion

Through a transformation of consciousness and a listening heart, locate yourself within the great drama of the universe and participate in creating a culture of hope, embedded in the dynamics of the cosmos and its unfolding into life.

With a deepened understanding of Earth as a living organism, discover a context in which life can be lived in a more meaningful way, with a deepened sense of place, with increased insight into wisdom traditions to create and redesign our work to advance ecological justice, planetary peace, and personal and social liberation.

Part 4
Longing of the Divine

Canticle to the Divine

I will rise, I will rise.
In the lives of the people, I will rise.
In the lives of the people of this land,
I will rise, I will rise.
With the resurgence of Earth,
we will rise, we will rise.
With the spirit of the divine,
we will rise, we will rise.
In places of poverty,
there beats deep despair.
In beautiful lands, gardens of Eden,
are nations of martyrs
whose people are taking
the road to Golgotha.
The rich have been taking
the fruits of their labor,
the work of their hands.
With the cry of the crucified,
people and planet,
come down from the cross
of the army's oppression,
the cross of injustice,
the cross of despair,
of violent homes,
of enduring illness,
of wages too meagre,
of forests turned wasteland.
Come down from the cross,
let there be no more martyrs.
Let us rise, let us rise.
Sing a song of resurgence.

Welcome this Easter:
economic justice,
planetary peace,
rights for all creatures,
wholeness of land,
of all God's creation.
Let there be a New Easter,
Fresh hope, celebration,
joy and of longing,
of Paschal liberation
everywhere, everywhere.

Toward a Spectrum Theology

Deep within the heart of the universe resides a profound inclination to commune, to be at one with, and to heal the great emptiness and abyss that exists at the edge of soul, life, and Earth. It is an inclination to flow with the pulsating presence of the divine, a shimmering presence that mysteriously invites us into the depths of our longing for self, life, Earth, and our God.

The longing of the divine includes the perceptions of a spectrum of contemplative, liberation, and creation theology. It provides the spiritual basis for nurturing a mystical and engaged cosmology. The practice of a spectrum theology involves:

- A literacy of the heart: an awareness of one's intrapsychic depths, interiority, and identity that extends to embrace the universe (contemplation)
- A literacy of society: a critical comprehension of social, cultural, political, and economic dynamics that embraces also the other-than-human world (liberation)
- A literacy of Earth: a capacity to understand the functions of the cosmos and to listen to the voices of Earth that is accompanied by moments of awe, wonder, and mystery (creation)

Contemplation reflects on the interdependence of all things and communes with cosmic forces to empower action.

Liberation attends to the plight of the poor and shows us that our quest is for the freedom not only of humanity but of all creation.

Creation presents the challenge to heal ecological devastation, while celebrating the entire universe as "the place that bears God's signature," manifest in the divine beauty and sacred mystery that is everywhere.

This new literacy will enhance our visionary and prophetic ability to celebrate and transform our experience of soul, life, and Earth, resulting in a hope-filled future that views each moment as revelatory and an encounter with the divine.

A Vast Spectrum

I wish and hope the fragments of this journey
interact and blend in a spectrum of identity and
    delight.
May they flow together in harmony
on this silent palmetto morning.
May each fragment of belief
become a song of broken beauty,
echoing forth from the heart of the cosmos.

Sacredness and Depth

The call of our generation is to discover the evolutionary role of religion.

Deep within the soul lies a longing for the divine, a relentless longing, for a life that is fresh, new, and original. This longing confronts us with choices and the promise of fresh hope and possibility as we strive to avoid the terrible risk of an unlived life. In our hunger for belonging, we become increasingly enveloped in the mysterious presence of the divine.

Deep within the heart of the universe there is a profound inclination to commune, to be at one with, to heal the emptiness and abyss that reside in the enduring desire for relationship and oneness. Relationships receive their vitality from within the recesses at the edge of the soul, life, Earth, and the divine origins of all that is.

The pulsating presence of the divine hovers over all creation and permeates each particle. This presence draws us into the depths of our longing and evokes the wonder and awe that activate the spontaneity of the soul. As we follow the relentless invitation to create a new culture out of the fusion of cosmic consciousness and social forms, we discover our identity in relationship to each other, the planet, and our God.

A burgeoning spirituality is rising from the story of soul retrieval, of bringing the soul of a people and a culture back to life. It is a story of reversing the mechanistic materialism that has reduced Earth to dirt and the people to machines. It is a new story of reclaiming, a story of fresh appreciation for the beauty of a landscape—a story celebrated in songs, poetry, and music. It is a story of vitality and depth, of bringing back the soul of the cosmos, a story of divine presence and a newfound freedom for communities everywhere.

This new spirituality is unprecedented in human history. It is a spirituality of longing, energized by the determination of a people and the impulse of the planet to discover new freedom and new psychic depths. With this fresh perspective, we can learn to live in an organic, unfolding world. We can see that the dynamics of destruction and creation are woven into the very fabric of existence. This emerging spirituality is the spirituality of the planet itself; it is increasingly the sign of a new Paschal moment, of hope for the world.

In this new Easter epoch, we can experience a spirituality of longing for life, a spirituality that hears the cry of the poor and sees in the raped rain forest, the abused spouse, and the abandoned child a sacrament, a special presence of God. It is a spirituality that perceives the cross in a natural gas pipeline on native ground, the denial of rights to a river, the murder of young school children. It is a spirituality that calls out for justice to heal the wounded soul of a people, and the violence perpetrated against Earth.

A resurrection spirituality is being born out of this cosmic Paschal moment, a sign and the midwife of new life for the planet and its peoples. It is a resurging spirituality, empowered by an Easter energy, marked by a converging concern for the restoration of Earth, the restructuring of society, and care of the soul.

Emerging from this Paschal moment is a new perspective on relationship to soul, life, Earth, and God, a new energy of freedom and fulfillment for the planet and every species. It is an energy generated by the reality of human suffering and planetary pain, an energy that sees cosmic significance in awakening to the presence of a starving child and the abused Earth as the threshold of a new Exodus event, a new moment of solidarity.

At this Easter moment, the poor speak to us in many voices. As we listen to the cry of the poor and the cry of Earth, we begin to understand from a personal and a planetary perspective that the poor are the sacrament of God and they have lessons to teach us. The poor make up two-thirds of the world's population, which demonstrates that the hallmark of our times is poverty. It follows that our capacity to live a preferential option for poor people and the poor Earth is the starting point for a new and authentic spirituality that begins at the edge of our longings: the longings of soul, life, Earth, and God.

The Cry for a New Creation

As we answer the call to justice, we realize that we are a people with shifting cosmologies, changing stories, striving to heal the separateness between the spirit and the street, vision and despair, this magnificent planet and our inadequate theologies. As I journey through this time, I find that it helps me to keep my bearings if I look at the process through the lens of the incarnation.

For me, the incarnation is not just an event that happened two thousand years ago, as it certainly did. It is the ongoing outburst of life we see when the sun comes up in the morning, when the flower blooms, when the child is born, when an idea emerges in our imagination, or when instinct or impulse calls people together. These are all incarnational moments, a time in which the living God is made visible among us.

With this perspective, the cross can be understood beyond the historical Good Friday. Within the cosmic crucifixion, reside the Gethsemane moments of a wasted life, of enduring poverty, of depleted resources, of an extractive economy, of a politics ruled by greed and special interests, of a despair that permeates the soul of our youth, of the hunger for meaning that exists within all our hearts.

So too the resurrection, our Easter, becomes an ongoing event. It happens when we become one with our God, with our loved ones, and with our Earth. It happens through moments of surprise, in times of prayer when we move from illusion to reality. When we realize that prayer is not as much about petition or contrition as about celebration and praise, about aligning ourselves with the unfolding of life, rather than asking God to make the world the way we would like it to be. We make our Easter with

Earth not just at the spring equinox but when our lives and our gatherings create an experience of communion that is alive and full.

Pentecost transcends the historical event that happened fifty days after Easter and resulted in the birth of the church. We celebrate a planetary Pentecost that continues to happen among us—in the moments when all creation experiences harmony, balance, and peace, when the Earth community is involved in reciprocity and transformation. Pentecost happens when the creative energy of the divine permeates the natural world and animates the landscape of our souls, when we become one with God, with the planet, with ourselves and with each other, when everything is sacred and sacramental.

Our traditions tell us that we are to be engaged in a resacralization of life, a new Exodus moment, a new era, a planetary Pentecost. When we view the planet as the body of the wounded and risen Christ, we celebrate both the struggle and the hope that will take us forward into the future. It is said that hope is the oxygen of the soul. Hope is experienced in the struggle, not in the victory. Hope is the conviction that tomorrow can be different from today.

There is an alignment between the biblical story of the Exodus and the moment we are living now. The new story does not replace the Christian story, it ennobles it, empowers it, and gives it greater depth, context, and meaning. For me, the Exodus is what Thomas Berry calls the movement from the Cenozoic era into the postindustrial Ecozoic era, a more mutually enhancing context for life. The transition from a time of Earth destruction to a time when humanity has a new role to play is unprecedented in history. We now have responsibility for the viability of this planet.

The Role of Mysticism

This new understanding of the place we humans fill in the web of life requires that we become engaged mystics. Mysticism is a unitive experience. One of the things about past religious practices is that they have often taught us morality without mysticism. We've been told what rules to keep but have not been encouraged to experience the divine in order to energize and nourish our souls. Without such experiences, we lack the moral courage and critical consciousness that can empower us to do justice. Justice making without mysticism becomes plodding. It is obligation without celebration. Thomas Berry encouraged us with these words:

> When overwhelmed by the magnitude of the task before us in our work for the human community or for the entire Earth community, we might look out over the fields to the blue expanse of the heavens, to the clouds in the sky, to the meadows in blue. We might listen to the mockingbird, observe the bee or butterfly in flight. The flowers bloom, the birds sing, the rivers flow to the sea. Those same powers that give the sun its radiance and enable so many diverse life forms to fulfill their assigned tasks, those same powers support our work.

Mysticism is nourished by creation. If we were living on a lunar landscape, our souls would shrink, our spirituality would be diminished.

The mystical tradition will nourish us for the journey we have ahead. It is an unmediated relationship with God.

It can happen in your room, it can happen in the park, it can happen in your kitchen, it can happen in your encounter with your spouse or children, it can happen in a personal way.

Poverty and the Divine Presence

The mystics talk about the notion of breakthrough. Breakthrough doesn't mean that God wasn't there before, and when you have a breakthrough, God shows up. Rather, it means you are open to the divine presence in a new way. Gustavo Gutiérrez wrote about this in *Liberation Theology*: "When you take away the barriers, you can feel God's presence most fully." Poverty indicates the presence of the divine. Gutierrez asserted that God is more present in the poor, not because they are better, but because they are poor.

This is not a justification for poverty. There are reasons for poverty; economic structures can create poverty by their very nature. And some systems meant to relieve poverty are in some ways exploitative themselves. This awareness of the divine presence is in no way a reason not to work for justice and the eradication of poverty.

I See the Blood Upon the Rose

I see the blood upon the rose.
There is wisdom in these words.
Anguish and pain,
joy, sorrow and possibility.
I ask you, is not life a fusion
of joy and sorrow,
of beauty and brokenness,
fear of tomorrow and what's next?
Listen to your soul.
It tells tales of possibility.
Let the little ones speak.
Embrace the paradox of this journey.

Reflection at the Edge of the Divine

The focus of these reflections is to discover, explore, experience, and articulate a resonance between the passionate promptings of the heart of humanity and our relationship to soul, life, and creation through the genesis story, signs of the times, Earth literacy, social analysis, and theological reflection on our Christian tradition (operative theology). A mystical and engaged cosmology can be achieved when these components are understood within the ethical dynamics of the universe story as expressed in communion (everything is related), differentiation (no two things are the same), and interiority (each expression of creation has a unique identity and purpose).

The genesis story of the Hebrew Bible is the master narrative of the West. Its drama of loss and return to the garden has had a profound influence on our psyches, our culture, and our way of life.

We change farms into gardens, irrigate deserts more suitable for cactus to grow lawns. Our urge is driven by a desire to get back to the garden.

Theology has been shaped by this urge. Acts of acquisition and greed have been sanctioned as spiritual practices to enable us to get back to the garden.

A further extension is the doctrine of predestination popularly portrayed on bumper stickers as "He who dies with the most toys wins." We also know there is no correlation between the acquisition of wealth and possessions, and living a full and satisfied life.

The thesis of this book is that we need a new story, a new genesis: a story that is dynamic, interactive, and relational; a story that dissolves anthropocentrism, individualism, and greed; a story to enhance the work of partnership and justice, to eradicate systems of oppression; a story to nurture restoration and collaboration. This story will focus our destiny; enliven our hearts; and be attentive to the voices of creation, liberation, and contemplation.

The New Cosmology: Earth Literacy

Our cosmology is our worldview, our story. It responds to the key questions of our lives: "Where did I come from?" "Who am I?" and "Where am I going?" Through our cosmology, we reflect on the origins and unfolding of the universe and our place within it. Properly understood and reflected on, our story makes possible an emotional, aesthetic, and spiritual fulfillment; it weaves together an interconnected web of the universe, Earth, life, and consciousness.

Through Earth literacy, we are able to recognize the story and our place in it. This new story shed light on our tradition and energizes our quest to discover our place and participation in the great work, the historical mission of humanity at this time.

When we begin to appreciate the new cosmology, we become aware in a new way that the sound of the wind, the songs of the bird, the beauty of a flower, the mysteries of dawn and dusk are revelatory, and each is a sacred moment of divine disclosure. When we remember our early years and our early encounters with creation, we understand these experiences as a primary sacrament—sacred moments that contain the seeds of our calling and the context of our place in the great work.

When we liberate ourselves from the book-bound world, we feel empowered and discover more fully our identity and purpose. With symbol, gesture, and sound, we respond to the awesome beauty of creation and realize anew that we have become literate in the language of Earth. Earth literacy becomes a moment of grace: a conscious experience of unity; an awakening to a deep presence of the sacred; an engagement with beauty; a threshold to divine mystery, to the language of divinity that speaks of sacredness and soul.

Cosmologist Brian Thomas Swimme proposes that our moment is a time to discover the creative dynamics of the universe and become engaged in a mutually enhancing process.

Cultural Moment: The Signs of the Times

Each of us is born into a particular moment in history; our lives are profoundly impacted by the times in which we live. My life was affected by the civil rights movement, Vatican II, the Vietnam war, and the therapeutic revolution of the sixties and seventies. The pioneering efforts of Sr. Gail Worcello, CP, and Bernadette Bostwick, CP, to build an Ecozoic monastery in the Green Mountains of Vermont, for example, grew out of an awareness of the new universe story. If this were the Middle Ages, their work would predictably have been education, health care, or social work.

Our work is not only influenced by the cultural moment, we are also influenced by cosmological forces. Thomas Berry referred to this when he wrote that humanity's historical mission is influenced by those "overarching movements that give shape and meaning to the larger destinies of the universe."

During Vatican II, a defining phrase was incorporated into the document on *The Church in the Modern World*: "the signs of the times." Attributed to Josef Cardinal Suenens and MD Chenu, OP, this phrase refers to the "expectations, longings and characteristics" of a particular cultural moment and the challenges this moment presents. Reading the signs of the times involves understanding historical events as moments of divine communication. Through our reflection, we gain insight into how to reformulate our tradition in response to the needs and expectations of the modern world, and to view each particular moment as an opportunity for transformation and as a moment of grace.

Sacrament

Every word is a sacrament,
an infusion of wisdom and possibility.
Every breath an inhalation
and exhalation of existence.

Let my soul speak,
activate the overflowing beauty
of this sacred moment.

Listen to the pulse of the planet,
embrace the soul of the cosmos,
as each new moment punctuates
the heartbeat of the universe.

Social Analysis

A mystical and engaged cosmology will be nourished by our capacity to become literate in relation to the social dynamics of our lives; this is understood as social analysis. The great cultural workers of our era were aware of the need to penetrate the mystification of society and see clearly the needs and responses required.

Saul Alinsky, the architect of community organization, was called the therapist of the apathetic. He was convinced that we need to be able to penetrate our social reality, to move beyond seeing that either there is no problem or that problem is so overwhelming we can't do anything about it. His work was directed at assisting people to recognize their powerlessness and begin to act with increased freedom, dignity, and self-esteem.

Paulo Freire, the Brazilian prophet of popular education, was called the vagabond of the obvious. His work focused on inculcating critical awareness so people could understand the dynamics of their oppression and engage in acts of transformation. The practice of social analysis involves reflecting on the congruence and contradictions of how we see the world and its relationship to our practice in regard to society, ecology, culture, and economics.

You can begin this exploration by reflecting on a commodity that you own (i.e., an article of clothing). As you read the label, explore the following questions:

- Who made it?
- Where was it produced?
- How was it distributed?
- Who made a profit?

- Who makes decisions about its manufacture and marketing?

Social analysis can assist our movement toward a mystical and engaged cosmology by helping us examine what a product says about our lifestyle and our life. We achieve this by raising questions about society and seeking answers, which involves critical awareness and the work of justice.

An Operative Theology

A challenge for the believing community is to examine our Christian tradition in light of the universe story. This new perspective will be accomplished by examining our history.

Our Christian story begins with the Book of Genesis, where we read about the idyllic time in the Garden of Eden, a time of freedom and perfection. The story continues with Abraham, Sarah, Moses, and the prophets, where we read of chaos, the fall, and the promise of a redeemer.

The New Testament recounts the Christ event. We recount the birth, life, death, and resurrection of Jesus the Christ. The Christ events culminate in Pentecost and the coming of the Kingdom, the reign of God. The New Testament ends with the Book of Revelation, the Second Coming, when there is a return to the garden, to a second moment of idyllic presence and perfection.

The challenge before us today is to view this inherited tradition within a cosmological context: a context that includes chaos, violence, and creativity. From the perspective of cosmology, suffering, death, age, we see that destruction and creation are integral to existence; they are not to be redeemed from but are rather to be embraced as the "bitter and burdensome" components of existence.

Within the context of the new story, we see how our Christian roots can provide a fresh perspective on our spiritual journey. For example, we see that the exodus of the Hebrew Bible is more than the liberation of a people through the Red Sea to the promised land. It is also a continuing event, an evolving process by which the human community and the other-than-human world participate in a second exodus—an ongoing departure from the terminal phase of the geological/biological era of the Cenozoic to the emerging Ecozoic era, a new time when humans will be present to creation in a more mutually enhancing way.

In a similar way, the Paschal mystery of Jesus' incarnation, death, and resurrection leading to the Pentecost is a new story for our time, a great narrative whereby we see the incarnation in the birth of a flower, the dawn of a day, and the life of a child. The crucifixion becomes a cosmic event understood as the death of a rain forest, the poverty of a people, the devastation of the planet. Resurrection becomes the beginning of spring, the birth of a movement, the unleashing of an imagination, and the inception of a program about to unfold.

Central to the Christian story is the notion of the reign of God over the Kingdom: that moment when justice will reign on Earth. From a cosmological perspective, I envision a world of geo-justice and engaged cosmology, a time when harmony, balance, and peace are palpable and present on the planet. These theological reflections are intended to extend our reflection to embrace the dynamics of the universe and to celebrate our Christian tradition from a cosmological perspective, seeing each of these themes as a moment of grace, an opportunity for transformation and change.

Base communities in liberation theology and programs in field education have developed a process called *operative theology*. This is the movement from orthodoxy to orthopraxis. As children, we were taught our catechism. It contained the credal statements that summarized our belief system, we learned the Ten Commandments, the seven sacraments, and who God is.

Today we are being invited to describe and articulate the core beliefs of our tradition as our operative theology. In other words, what in all of our belief system motivates us to live our gospel of life?

An operative theology asks, "What are the deepest convictions, the visceral responses that guide my life and have their roots in my tradition?" Theological reflection provides increased insight into our tradition and reveals new possibilities for creative action in the world.

I recall a story told by Rene Fumoleau, OMI, an Oblate priest from France, who, after completing his studies, was assigned to work with the Dene people in Canada's Northwest Territories. He spent his first days in Yellowknife, conducting classes on all the major tenets of the faith. He wanted to share with his new community all that he had learned in his theological studies.

When he concluded his classes, he posed a question to the people: "What of all that I have taught you is the most important aspect of the Christian faith?"

The answer came back: "Never lock your door!"

The operative theology of the Dene people was hospitality. They knew that in the frigid cold of the North, the most important gesture they could express to their neighbor was the opportunity of getting out of the cold.

In light of this story and your own, what is your operative theology?

What Do I Trust Is True?

Life begins with trust, openness, peace, acceptance.
Creation is about being held, beauty, change, tears, letting
    go, homecoming.
Let it be.
Connectedness is celebration, laughing out of control,
    playing, dancing, storytelling, mutuality, abundant
    food.
Say yes to life, gratitude.
Say yes to death.
Say yes to mystery, to labor pains, to new birth, to
    compassion.

Revisioning Roots

Where does religious tradition fit in our developing picture of creativity, belonging, wholeness, and soul work? I return again and again to this question: "What is it that I believe?" Or, in the language of Sallie McFague, "What is my credo?" I often phrase this question: "What do I trust?"

Trust is a better word than *believe* for this purpose: belief is cognitive, but trust is affective. When we ask what we trust, one way of finding an answer is to ask another question: "What is it that I'm not anxious about? What is it that doesn't make me nervous?" For each of us, a core conviction grounds us that is visceral and rooted in certainty. One of the challenges in dealing with our tradition is that sometimes our operative theology, our deep core convictions, seems at odds with our inherited tradition. The result is that we feel stifled and stuck.

As we have seen through theological reflection, we can discover an alignment between the truth that is revealed in our hearts and what we have learned from our inherited traditions. It is a search for congruence. If we go deep enough into our own psychic passageways and deep enough into our tradition, we meet that underground river which is the divine, and there we find the congruence of our operative theology.

An operative theology within the context of the universe story makes links between the new cosmology and our inherited tradition. On the basis that all theology is contextual, we ask where the divine and the human fit in, what the meaning of justice is. In our questioning, we are reminded that we must look at history from the point of view of those who suffer and are oppressed.

We are challenged also to realize that the energy for justice flows from our experience of the divine, as encountered by humanity and in the natural world. With this consciousness, we appreciate how Francis of Assisi spoke of Brother Sun and Sister Moon.

Universe as Primary Revelation

The new cosmology reveals our present understanding of the universe as unfolding in time and interconnected through a common origin. A functional cosmology supports a world of harmony, balance, and peace and is predicated on a worldview that resonates with the dynamics of the unfolding universe. A mystical and engaged cosmology can be understood as an operative theology within the context of the universe.

In this way, our theological reflection becomes meta-religious. It includes the wisdom that is available through other avenues of thought and reflection. A mystical and engaged cosmology includes:

- Reading the signs of the times of this cultural moment
- Earth literacy and the new cosmology
- Social analysis and critical awareness
- Theological reflection and an operative theology
- Ethical principles of the universe

A mystical and engaged cosmology includes an articulation of those spontaneous tendencies that spring forth from the human heart and find expression in a worldview that is at once functional and a vehicle for justice.

Our approach to the experience and practice of an operative cosmology includes the following approaches:

Freedom. Freedom is the capacity and willingness to think outside the box and become liberated from any tendency toward internalized oppression.

Hope. Hope is the oxygen of the soul, the virtue of tomorrow. Children are the archetypes of hope and sacramental signs that tomorrow can be better than today.

Intuition. Intuition is the capacity to be open to surprise, to unleash our imagination, and to embrace the moment of the unexpected.

Curiosity. Curiosity opens us to events, insights, and initiatives that can shed light on our lives and open us to the possibility of a new consciousness. Being curious leads us to let go of the present awareness that holds us back and keeps in place a dysfunctional cosmology.

Initiative. Initiative is the capacity for creative action and can be evoked by trusting the sacred impulse.

Transformative action. Transformative action is the ability to create a better world for the children. Through transformative action, what is written in the stars and practiced in the street is inscribed in the DNA of our soul.

In summary, a mystical and engaged cosmology connects the heart of humanity to the heart of the cosmos. It nurtures gestures of spontaneity and beauty manifest in the verdant forests, the azure waters, the song of the skylark, and the radiant glow of snow-capped mountains, along with clean water, nutritious food, healthy children, and a new soul for society populated by a new people who are discovering what it means to be human in an unfolding universe. This meta-religious experience is a celebration of the realization that the primary manifestation of the divine is in the cosmological order.

In this way we begin to see that cultural moment, signs of the times, Earth literacy, new story, social analysis, theological reflection, and the ethical principles embedded in the universe as contributing components of a mystical and engaged cosmology, culminating in a new Ecozoic event, a meta-religious movement for our time.

You can do the following:

- Name your deepest concern. What most deeply touches your heart and calls you to work for a better world?
- Name the current cosmology. What are the characteristics of the current cosmology that hold the dysfunction in place?
- Name the prophets. Who are the prophetic voices of yesterday and today that you hear and read, whose voices are aligned to your own and speak to your heart?
- Find the roots of your tradition. Name your operative theology and indicate how it is the primary motivating force that guides your actions in the world and finds its source in your deepest conviction.
- Tell your personal story. How does your story nurture or resist the advent of a fully functional cosmology? What practices of creativity and unselfconsciousness could liberate you from the oppressive elements of your story?
- Reflect on the ethical principles of the universe. How do communion (compassion), differentiation (creativity), and interiority (transformation) contribute to the practice of a functional cosmology and support the alignment between consciousness (awareness) and conscience (actions in the world)?

From the Stars to the Street

The challenge of engaged cosmology is to make hidden connections, to bring together the stars and the street. This involves bringing together in our awareness and our action the relationship between the stars and the street. Our role in these in-between times is to become hospice workers for structures and forms that need to die with dignity and to become midwives for the new forms that need to be born. Like blades of grass that burst forth from the brittle and broken concrete that form our sidewalks and highways, we are challenged to break through the brittleness of a calcified culture and to act in unprecedented ways. We are challenged to become bridge builders to heal the separation between the world as it is and the world as we would like it to be: to connect the stars to the street.

As creators of hidden connections, we become aware of the stark signs of a withering and destructive society and the second superpower that is emerging from the streets of your city or town. Like stars, we come to illuminate a horizon of hope.

As prophetic voices of hidden connections, we experience a fresh realization that our address for a life of accomplishment and fulfillment does not reside on Wall Street, Bay Street, Pennsylvania Avenue, 10 Downing Street, or Parliament Hill but rather at the intersection of mysticism and engagement. It is this address that can unite the stars to the street and become the birthplace of an engaged cosmology. This is where our emerging awareness and prophetic action become one act—an act of engaged cosmology that unites the stars to the street.

Story: Narrative Cosmology

The work of an engaged cosmology can be enveloped in a membrane of story. We understand the universe and our place within it.

As we ponder the beginnings of the universe and the transformational events that have taken place over time, we discover who we are and experience a deeper moment of identity and destiny.

It is by knowing and reflecting on our own story within the context of the great cosmic unfolding that we can achieve a new self-awareness: an awareness that provides stability in a sea of social chaos.

As we discover and tell our story and view it within the context of the great story, we begin to see our role and place in the beautiful new world about to be born in our midst.

A world of wisdom is gained through listening, difference without exile, and community without cooptation.

Generosity, Sacrifice, and Reciprocity

An engaged cosmology evokes and celebrates the enduring tendency and predisposition for the universe and humanity to engage in the dynamic process of self-transcendence. The universe reminds us of the generosity and the capacity to go beyond itself. The sun constantly gives of itself, providing light and warmth to the planet; this expression of generosity is accompanied by moments of enormous sacrifice. The entire drama of the universe story is a reminder of the gift of self: the galaxies give birth to planets; hydrogen and oxygen surrender to make water. Creation and destruction are a constant cadence in the unfolding universe.

In a parallel way, humanity from time to time embraces a wondrous quality; it goes beyond survival and selfishness and demonstrates episodic transformations of the spirit.

These moments of sacrifice, so profoundly present in the cosmos, are also present when people participate in the work of personal, social, and ecological transformation.

This quality of generosity and sacrifice is required to make the transition into a more just world. Generosity and sacrifice make possible not only a better world but a world of beauty, a place where sacredness and divinity permeate each moment of existence.

The process of moving toward a more human world and healthy planet includes liberating not only the oppressed but also the oppressor. This process includes an awareness that the liberator contains elements of oppression, and at the same time, the oppressor is in some way a force for freedom.

Interrelatedness and Communion

A great lesson of the universe is that inseparability is a governing principle of life. We are born of the universe to commune with all creation.

Conscious that relatedness and community are the basis of our being, we joyfully realize that self-discovery is only fully possible when we enter into and experience community.

As we look to the stars, we discover that the universe is a sacred community, and our existence is most fully understood when we are enveloped within a constellation of relationships. When we are present to each other in mutually enhancing ways, when we are present to each other in community, when we realize that we are all members of the Earth community and inevitable partners in an enormous Noah's ark of life, we realize our identity as members of the human family.

This experience of being present to each other strengthen us. It helps us realize anew that alienation, exile, loneliness, and separation are products of a cultural pathology. With this in mind, we realize that our desire for and tendency toward relationship with soul, life, Earth, and God are supported and empowered by both our deepest intuitions and the universe itself.

An Engaged Cosmology

Over the years, I puzzled about how to connect the wisdom of the prophetic cultural workers of the past with the new story of the universe. I was convinced that the imagination and processes of those whose work I'd known and studied were embedded in the paradigms of the past. In this way, I experienced a dualism between my past efforts and current engagement in the new cosmology.

That led me to articulate what I called *geo-justice*. I viewed this as the process of taking up the personal and planetary challenge of weaving together into a unified tapestry, a seamless garment of social and ecological justice. This approach involves exploring the dynamics of the universe as manifest in the three principles of differentiation, communion, and interiority. Geo-justice not only explores these principles but shows us how to incarnate them in cultural form. To do this, we need to view differentiation as local, communion as global, and interiority as psychosocial.

Through applying the approaches of community organization and development and conscientization at the local level, I developed a deeper understanding of difference and its implication for the work of geo-justice as it relates to race, gender, and class. Simultaneously, the work of global education and the meaning of global citizenship illuminated the cultural implications of communion. To explore the implications of interiority, I turned to the work of Carl Jung and Stan Grof and their understanding of the galaxies within, and I saw that the psyche (interior life) is coexistent with the universe itself, as it relates to body, mind, and spirit.

As I looked to the Christian tradition, I explored the meaning of the three principles from a trinitarian perspective. Differentiation as the source of uniqueness and difference becomes the Creator/God, often known as the Father. Similarly, communion as the source of relationship and interconnectedness is understood as spirit, commonly named Holy Spirit. Interiority takes on the perspective as the source of the word, which we normally call the Son.

I proposed that when these principles, now understood in trinitarian form, become present, divinity becomes palpable and present in our midst. Thus, the work of geo-justice not only brings harmony, balance, and peace to our planet but also evokes and celebrates a deeper awareness and experience of Cod.

What remained to be understood in this approach was the worrisome awareness that the method implemented to translate the components of geo-justice into cultural form was still immersed in the Newtonian-Cartesian paradigm. To translate geo-justice fully into the work of an engaged cosmology requires that we explore and make connections between the deep wisdom of the cultural workers of the past and the insights of the new story.

This approach raises many questions, but it also provides the opportunity to discover the deep cosmological connection present in the actual processes and approaches of cultural workers. This approach will heal any division between the focus of geo-justice and the practices involved in translating into cultural form the components of geo-justice—namely, differentiation (local-creator), communion (global-spirit), and interiority (psycho-social-word).

The work of engaged cosmology weaves together a connection between the stars and the street, what is most prophetic in cultural transformation, and the dynamics and power of an unfolding universe.

Action that emerges from a synthesis of contemplative, liberation, and creation spirituality understood within the context of the universe is constitutive of an engaged cosmology. An integral practice of dream, soul work, and action is the necessary condition for prolonged participation in engaged cosmology.

Creative Energy

Creative energy is the source from which we can harness the divine inclination toward transformation and new life. This divine creative energy sustains us in our work to bring forth a world of harmony, balance, and peace, a world that is mutually enhancing for people and the planet. An engaged cosmology empowers people to achieve their fondest desire for their lives and life on Earth—a world marked by dignity, security, meaning, purpose, happiness, and peace. This world can best be marked by naming itself as a revolution of the soul.

The Quest for an Engaged Cosmology

The vision of geo-justice and the work of the new cosmology provide a fresh perspective through the practice of a preferential option for Earth. Understanding the seamless garment of human poverty and ecological devastation, we act with Earth in mind.

If all our actions are not guided by an awareness of Earth, we are in danger of acting in such a way that we contribute to the oppression of the planet and the increased devastation of its people.

Reflecting on the genesis story, reading the signs of the times, Earth literacy, social analysis, operative theology, and approaches to an operative cosmology and geo-justice led me to pursue an understanding of what I called *engaged cosmology.* The questions became:

- How do we discover new and historical approaches to cultural transformation and the practice of geo-justice that will make balance, harmony, and peace possible?
- How do we align our initiatives toward cultural transformation with the dynamics operative in the universe?

With this in mind, we can accomplish our actions without any separation between culture and the cosmos. The result will be a dynamic integration between the actions we undertake and the patterns in place in the universe itself. Every initiative, every action, every spirituality, and cosmology are contextual; they originate and flow from an awareness of both the universe and the cultural moment.

With the cosmos as a next contact for spirituality, we can address the challenges of our future. Engaged cosmology includes retrieving the eternal wisdom distilled from the cultural workers of the past and aligning this legacy with the dynamics of an unfolding universe. From this perspective, I celebrate the connection between the stars and the street and discover anew the possibility of an engaged cosmology.

Naming an Engaged Cosmology

At this moment of destruction and decline, we search for a new identity and ability to act. When we become consciously attuned to the dynamics of the universe and act in alignment with this awareness, we can discover an engaged cosmology.

Engaged cosmology is an immersion into the deep creative powers of the universe and the most direct contact a human can have with the divine.

Engaged cosmology is a new context for our journey, a place for our longings where poet and politician are one, a cosmic journey of struggle and fulfillment.

Engaged cosmology is where we embrace intimacy and contemplation, communion and solitude, inwardness and prophetic action, impulse and practice, mystery and engagement, cultural work and cosmic consciousness.

The hunger for sacredness and depth resides in soul, life, and Earth. This hunger is healed, responded to, and nourished by an experience of the divine as we participate in a mystical and engaged cosmology.

Engaged cosmology is a process and a pattern that finds expression in story, generosity, transcendence, children and interrelatedness, creative energy, magnanimity, liberation, self-healing, originating energy and the sacred impulse, cosmic dynamics, geo-justice, consciousness and cultural genesis, the heart of the universe and a listening heart, and interdependence and rootedness.

In an engaged cosmology, we awaken to the creative energy that streams through the cosmos. We understand that our role is to give this energy focus and expression.

An engaged cosmology enhances our ability to act. We are aware that the creative energy of the universe is pulsating through our lives and activating every aspect of our being.

We fulfill our destiny and participate in the transformation of a broken world when we engage in this work.

An engaged cosmology reveals new insights into the great cultural workers of the past when we view their practice through the lens of the universe.

An engaged cosmology nurtures a critical reflection that gives expression to a deep cosmic longing that calls us to heal what is broken and transform the face of Earth as we strive to make all things new.

An engaged cosmology challenges us to transform our consciousness and our conscience. We are invited to weave together webs of wisdom and programs of action. As we honor the aspirations of the heart, we rediscover the God of the universe and set our sails toward a hope-filled future.

Principles and Themes for an Engaged Cosmology

Principles of an engaged cosmology include:

- Generosity and self-transcendence
- Restorative properties and the self-healing resurgence of the soul
- Evolutionary freedom within a vast unfolding universe to liberate the planet
- Celebration of sacredness and culture, moments of divine presence
- Gratitude, hope, beauty, and wisdom always at the threshold of something new
- The great story and the transformational events of our lives, told both by the stars and the street, that weave together membranes of meaning.
- Cosmic creation and destruction embedded within the Bethlehem, Gethsemane, and Easter moments of grace

The following twelve themes were discovered through reflecting on the connections between the wisdom and practice of cultural workers of the past and an awareness of the dynamics of an unfolding universe, as described in the works on new cosmology.

Magnanimity and the liberation of creation. Engagement in deep cultural work nourishes a magnanimity of spirit. In the process, we experience a felt sense of oneness with the universe and all that is. Our engagement inspires a deep communion with humanity and the other-than-human world. We transcend narrow self-interest and are moved to grant each member of the

Earth community the freedom to inhabit the planet and fulfill its role. We are inspired by the generosity demonstrated by the self-giving of the sun.

Self-healing and the soul. Prophetic cultural change contains a healing dimension: when properly supported and stimulated, both Earth and psyche demonstrate self-healing properties. In each case, the cultural worker or cosmologist is more a witness than an agent.

Originating energy and the sacred impulse. The process of cultural transformation finds its direction and energy in responding to the felt sense of a sacred impulse that prompts our action, an impulse we understand as the continuing expression of the originating energy that gave birth to the universe and continues to support our efforts and intuition.

Cosmic dynamics and geo-justice. The harmony, balance, and peace embedded in the universe find their cultural manifestation in the work of geo-justice. In this process, beauty shines forth and divinity becomes palpable in our midst, as we celebrate communion (global), differentiation (local), and interiority (psycho-social) in cultural form.

Consciousness and culture. Engaged cosmology is an irreversible process that weaves together our cultural work with an awareness of the unfolding universe. We experience the support and interaction of consciousness and conscience. Our cosmological consciousness and our awareness of the world community create an integral presence. The result is that we act in accordance with what we see, and our cultural work evolves and unfolds in a manner consistent with the evolving universe.

Creation, destruction, and the dynamics of rebirth. Cultural work involves the capacity to die to oneself and rise to the concern for the other. These deep dynamics of creation, destruction, and rebirth are embedded in the process of life and in the dynamics of our traditions. They find expression in the epiphanies (incarnation), Gethsemane moments (cross), and inevitable outpouring of new life in the larger arc of existence (resurrection).

Narrative and the great unfolding. A profound and appropriate approach to our cultural work is the practice of storytelling. Each story heard, told, and celebrated is perceived as a paragraph in the great sacred story and a context that inevitably prompts us into action to resacralize our lives and the meaning of existence. Our stories, told within the context of the great story, create action to transform the world.

The heart: Listening to the universe. Deep listening is a practice that resonates in the recesses of the cultural worker. It is understood as an echo from the pulsating heart of the universe. Listening to the other and to the heart of the universe creates a fabric of meaning and wisdom and fosters new moments of mutuality for Earth and every species.

Roots of engagement. An engaged cosmology is rooted in a felt sense of interdependence (contemplation), a desire that all peoples be free (liberation), and a reverence for a resacralized Earth (creation).

The little ones. Deep cultural therapy focuses on the nurture, support, and protection of the little ones and unborn of every species. When we detach ourselves from the pain of the present moment, we experience an invitation to awaken the imagination of youth to provide both protection and a portal into the future.

Interrelatedness and communion. The cultural worker is a builder of community. The work is nourished and energized by inseparability and the desire to commune with all members of the community of life: the Noah's ark of existence. The cultural worker is drawn forth by longing to make belonging in the universe possible and by dissolving the separation, exile, alienation, and loneliness that prevent authentic relationships with soul, life, Earth, and the divine.

Creative energy and the celebration of uniqueness. The universe mirrors the divine act of creativity and participates in abundant acts of creativity and expressions of new life. Each person dances into the future with a unique capacity for creativity and celebration of new life.

A Cosmic and Cultural Convergence

An engaged cosmology will evoke and support the practice of generosity and big-heartedness. We realize deeply our interconnectedness. In a new moment of transformation, we are inspired to work for the liberation of all, to set the captives free.

An engaged cosmology accesses the emergent energy that breaks through and celebrates the beauty and exuberance of new life.

As we discover the dynamic connection between the stars and the street, we realize that the energy released in the process has self-healing properties. This primal energy first found its expression in the originating energy of the universe. Today it becomes a cleansing and protective source to dispel all doubt and despair and makes it possible for beauty to blossom forth.

A beauty that is present in relationship, in difference and in depth.

A beauty that blossoms forth in the land, in the soul of the people.

A beauty that is present in the child, palpable in the elder, that envelopes the landscape and the soul.

A beauty that draws us forward into a new moment of liberation, where we can sing with Nina Simone and so many others, "how it feels to be free!"

A beauty that shines forth like a blade of grass through broken pavement.

A beauty that calls forth fresh moments of hope, that is oxygen for the soul and is the conviction that something makes sense, regardless of how it turns out.

A beauty that evokes the practice of an engaged cosmology, that reminds us of our common origins and of the profound Paschal moments of Gethsemane and Easter.

A beauty that stirs the imagination and attunes us to hear the universal voice of vocation.

A beauty that invites us into a place of meaning, as we create together unforgettable membranes of meaning to nurture our journey and move us forward into the future.

A beauty that will nurture an engaged cosmology and empower us to transform the world through the balanced turbulence of intimacy and contemplation, mysticism, and action.

A beauty that invites us to celebrate new thresholds of possibility and hope, as we position ourselves at the doorway of

- Gratitude for the present
- Hope for tomorrow
- Appreciation of generosity
- Wonder of sacredness
- Alignment in wisdom

An engaged cosmology that unites the stars and the street reminds us of the deep connection between the universal wisdom revealed in the work of cultural transformation and the dynamic powers present in the unfolding universe. When a dynamic integration occurs between these two powers, an engaged cosmology blossoms forth.

The Dynamics of Engagement

Engaged cosmology is the contextual and culminating action that flows from a reflection that views the longing of soul as contemplation of the interdependence of the universe; the longing of life as liberation of the entire Earth community; the longing of Earth as a celebration of the awe, wonder, beauty, and pain of creation; and the longing of the divine as the unspoken hunger for sacredness and depth. These longings find expression in a spectrum theology that creates mutuality and alignment between the dynamics of the universe and strategic approaches to personal, social, and ecological transformation.

The primary portals of our development as a people are marked by relationships to soul, life, Earth, and divine. When we understand that these relationships are deepened and empowered by the desire, love, attraction, and longing that reside within the universe, we have entered the arena of an engaged cosmology.

Suddenly all divisions and dualisms are dissolved, all separations between religion and science, impulse and conscience, cosmology and cultural melt into a newfound oneness. We discover that all approaches and disciplines need each other. A fresh alignment between cosmic wisdom and the universality of cultural insight tumbles forth. We have discovered an engaged cosmology. The universal dynamics of cultural transformation and the principles operative in the universe coalesce into a new consciousness and new avenues of action.

Within this newfound fusion of cosmology and cultural action, we discover great joy and the possibility of empowerment.

The dialogue between culture and cosmology results in an architecture for change: an approach embedded in the cosmos, distilled from the theory and practice of deep cultural work, and responsive to needs of this particular cultural moment.

An engaged cosmology reduces the distance between the world as it is and the world as we would like it to be. It heals the disparity between our vision of a new humanity and the dysfunctional world in which we live. The manifestation of an engaged cosmology involves a continuing effort to discover the cultural implication of those tendencies that are deeply encoded in the human venture.

An engaged cosmology involves the dynamic integration of all that is beautiful, mysterious, and true. It weaves together into a harmonious tapestry the valued legacy of our religious traditions, the profound insights of the experience of soul, the practices of cultural transformation, and the mystery of the story of the universe. It is out of the interaction and distilled wisdom of these cascading revelations that a new world of unprecedented beauty can be called forth. It is a world manifesting value, meaning, and wonder, mediated by the revelatory impact of a new master narrative: the universe story.

The understanding of the universe and the practice of geo-justice are constitutive to an engaged cosmology and integral to what it means to be human.

Pathways to Wisdom

An engaged spirituality cosmology draws on a wisdom that is both ancient and new. From the deep wells of tradition, we gain access to the wisdom that resides in the recesses of the universe and our souls. Through engaged spirituality, we penetrate the profound mysteries embedded in existence and made palpably present through symbol, myth, and analogy. An engaged spirituality activates the imagination and reminds us of our kinship with all life and the beauty present in each relationship.

Engaged spirituality invites us to discover the membranes of meaning present in each new moment, to perceive each encounter as a threshold to sacredness. An engaged spirituality invites us to align our energies with the dynamics of an unfolding universe and to accomplish whatever needs to be done to nurture compassion and new life. An engaged spirituality creates a context for fresh pathways to wisdom that are mystical, poetic, and profoundly interrelated.

A spectrum theology of contemplation, liberation, and creation that names our relationship to soul, life, Earth, and divine within the context of the universe story informs an engaged spirituality.

Engaged spirituality empowers us to accomplish whatever needs to be done and to make it possible for depth, freedom, beauty, and compassion to shine forth. This practice includes:

- Generosity and genuine interest in the well-being of all

- The resurgence of fresh energy to make possible the manifestation of new life
- A celebration of and communion with the divine that is present in all things
- A realization that we are all shaped, formed, and genetically coded for gratitude, compassion, sacredness, and depth

Through an engaged spirituality, we participate in meaningful action that is congruent with our worldview, true to our vision of the future, aligned with the unfolding of our lives, creative and transformative for all, and mutually enhancing for the entire community of life.

The Promise

Energy rises.
Convergence in the sky.
Collaboration happens.
Culture becomes cosmic.
Spontaneity bursts forth.
Soul awakens.
An energetic ocean
pours forth onto humanity and Earth.
Intimacy and contemplation abound.
In the longing for mystery and communion,
a search for parallel approaches
reveals the promise of a better world.

A Better Tomorrow

We live today in a time when society is marked by indicators of withering and decay, a time when institutions oppose their original purposes, a time when the efforts of good people with the best of intentions often produce the opposite of their intended results.

Generous people are being called to create a context of support where their destinies are not defeated, to build a bridge into the future: a bridge of transition and change; a bridge of new eras, new paradigms, and a new worldview. It will be a time to create clusters of generosity where people gather and reflect on approaches that fulfill their deeper purpose and build a vibrant Earth community.

It is a time to evoke and articulate a vision of a better tomorrow, a time to compose and live out beatitudes for the new creation in order to heal the wounds of soul, society, and Earth.

Beatitudes for the New Creation

Blessed are the contemplatives:
they shall experience the longing of the soul.
Blessed are the liberators:
they shall experience the longing of life.
Blessed are the Earthlings:
they shall experience the longing of creation.
Blessed are those who long for God:
they shall experience the interdependence of
    contemplation,
      the freedom of liberation,
      the beauty of the new creation.

Prophetic Roots

Amidst volcanic eruptions resulting in rigidity of structures and a metastasized culture, sometimes referred to as a culture of death, fresh energy and a new moment have come upon us. The wisdom of the ages inscribed in the illumination of the mystics and the discoveries of modern science have converged. Unlike our ancestors affected by the industrial era, we are now discovering who we are. Humanity has awakened to its destiny and call.

Through the revelations of the Hubble telescope, the insights of Albert Einstein, the vision of Pierre Teilhard de Chardin, the ecological awareness of Thomas Berry, and the liberation theology of Ivone Gebara and Leonardo Boff, we are now able to locate ourselves in the great cosmic drama: we have discovered our story. It is a story told by a child, proclaimed by the beauty of creation. It enhances our faith traditions and is a new context for the great work we are called upon to undertake.

As we gaze upon the beauty resulting from the volcanic eruptions and the enchanting landscape of bushlands and beaches, of valleys and mountaintops, we ponder again the great history of the universe and reflect on our common origin. From this place, we know that we are all shaped and formed in that same primordial furnace. We feel energized again to endure the bitter and burdensome moments of life, the Gethsemane moments, as we engage in the Paschal mystery story of our time—in the life, death, and rebirth of our people and our planet here in the beauty of God's creation.

Reimagining Our Future

How are we related to life, to Earth, to the divine? How do we discover where we are and gain guidance for the future? How do we take up our roles to be leaders in the twenty-first century?

When our ancestors began their prophetic work, with its particular challenges, the times were different, and the great work of those moments was unique to the time.

As we review the accomplishments of the past, we realize there is much more to be accomplished.

- The industrial revolution changed the world.
- Conflict among nations has shifted from spears to nuclear bombs.
- Technology gave us great gifts and also unimagined destruction.
- Transportation has gone from the horse and buggy to jet planes.
- Communication has moved from courier pigeon to email.
- Agriculture has moved from family gardens to agribusiness.
- Health care has changed from family doctors to state-funded delivery systems.
- Education has moved from two-room schools to distance learning.
- Clothing has shifted from traditional habits to street clothes.
- Religion has gone from catechism to the cosmos.

We have moved from a time when our ancestors awoke in the morning and knew where they were to a time of cultural Alzheimer's, when people on the planet lose their way.

Today we are like the adopted young man in the northwest of the United States who, when he learned of his adoption, engaged in the task of discovering who his parents were. As a people, we enter a new moment of grace when we are working to discover our origins and direction into the future, our new story.

We honor our ancestors, express gratitude for this present moment, and look toward the future with anticipation and hope.

It is a future inscribed in each of our hearts and punctuated by our participation in the great work, our participation in mission.

It is a future incarnated in our commitment to partnership, participation, and protection.

It is a future that will be enhanced by our shared vision that nurtures dignity, identity, and respect.

It is a future energized by the awe and wonder of an unfolding universe.

It is a future that honors and celebrates tenderness and strength and is captured by the vision of a flower bursting through the concrete, bringing beauty to a place of neglect.

Contemporary Challenges

Our great work is revealed by the challenge to respond with courage and compassion to this unprecedented moment in human/Earth history.

Our call to the great work is born out of the wisdom of the medieval mystic Meister Eckhart, who named ministry as "whatever needs to be done."

Our call today is to embody and celebrate the Indigenous wisdom of people whose presence on the land reveals the new story in magnificent ways.

Our call is to become instruments of health and wholeness; it is an invitation to heal both the planet and ourselves. It is a call for pure water, clean air, healthy livestock, and a wholesome Earth.

Our call is to nurture and support the dignity of the child and the wisdom of the elder and to care for all of us who inhabit this sacred land.

Our call is for wisdom and depth: to teach our children the wonders of creation, to invite each child to look to the stars and remind them they behold the bonfire of their ancestors.

Our call is to perceive in the poor and forsaken as a special presence of the divine.

Our call is to engagement, to an engaged cosmology.

Our call is to retrieve and celebrate the wisdom of the entire community of life, to respond to the crises and challenges of our time, as we align our energy to the unfolding dynamics of the universe and become catalysts for justice in an uncaring world.

Our invitation is to realize again that our work is a significant paragraph in the great cosmic story—a story told in each of our lives and projects and heard daily through the stars and the streets.

Our invitation is to awaken again to the realization that where we stand determines what we see, and that our position on this planet is to stand with the children and the poor of every species on this sacred Earth.

We are here to celebrate a new invitation, to create membranes of meaning, and embrace a new cosmic vision that will include:

- Imagination and wisdom
- Courage and engagement
- Intimacy and contemplation
- Trust and equanimity within the turbulence of new life.

Catalysts for Justice

We are invited to hear and respond to the call of justice: to connect the stars to the street, to comprehend the connection between the crack in the ozone layer and the crack sold in the street.

It is an invitation to altruism and generosity.

It is a time to transcend narrow self-interest and be enchanted by the generosity of the sun, a time for bigheartedness.

It is a time for the magnanimity our hearts to open and our imagination to soar.

It is a time of interconnectedness and inter-being.

It is an invitation to experience freedom and volcanic eruptions of the soul as we set about letting all the captives free.

It is an invitation to resurgence and regeneration, where our collective work makes possible emergence, beauty, and new life.

It is an invitation to weave together a membrane of compassion that dispels despair and reignites the original fire, that illuminates the dark night of our cultural soul.

It is an invitation to a deep resonance with all of life when, with all artists, we share the profound experience of how it feels to be free.

It is an invitation to celebrate and realize that hope is not a conviction that something will turn out well but a deep certainty that something makes sense and is worth doing regardless of how it turns out.

Beatitudes for an Engaged Cosmology

Blessed are the hopeful:
they hold a promise of tomorrow.
Blessed are the courageous:
they embrace the challenge of today.
Blessed are the forgiving:
they are free of the burden of the past.
Blessed are the people of prolonged engagement:
they will create a better world for the children.
Blessed are the disappointed:
they will rise and anticipate a better day.
Blessed are the self-forgetful:
they will engage in a compassionate embrace.
Blessed are the flowers, bursting forth in the spring:
they will bring beauty to Earth.
Blessed are the children:
they will celebrate spontaneity and new life.
Blessed are the contemplatives:
they will embrace the universe as one.
Blessed are the liberators:
they will set all the captives free
Blessed are the creation-centered:
they will appreciate the awesomeness.
Blessed are the engaged mystics:
they will ignite afire on Earth
and unite the stars with the street.

Contemplation and the Divine: Action/ Reflection

How has a deepened awareness of the emergent universe, of humanity's struggle for freedom, and of the recesses of your own soul prepared you to participate in an engaged cosmology?

In light of a new understanding, what are your primary areas of concern for our planet here at the threshold of a new era?

What actions do you plan to undertake to bring peace, joy, and compassion to our world and every species?

We rediscover the divine as we:

- Engage in collaborative projects that are marked by reciprocity, mutuality, and a new level of community
- Support personal and planetary challenges that are holistic and visionary, leading to passionate and practical action to bring balance to relationships and liberation to Earth and every species
- Explore lifestyles that are increasingly congruent with the dynamics of the universe, that enhance an integral human presence
- Find cultural expression in creativity, compassion, and psychic depth that are ecologically aware; holistic; just; and born out of awe, wisdom, and radical amazement
- Discover and develop ways to engage in meaningful and collaborative action that is aligned to our worldview and vision of the future
- Act in ways that are congruent with the narrative of our lives and the unfolding story of the universe and culminate in creativity and transformation infused with cosmological wisdom

- Ponder deeply key questions that connect the heart of humanity to the heart of the cosmos to renew and inspire the soul as we prepare the transition into a new era of justice and planetary wisdom at this threatening moment in our history.
- Celebrate the three-dimensional journey that is personal, communal, and cosmic
- Respond to those inclinations, hunches and intuitions that ignite our imaginations and summon us to engage in a spiritual journey grounded in our origins and marked by the touchstone categories of reciprocity, information, support, and common action
- Journey to the edge of our longing and heal our hunger for sacredness and depth as we create together a planetary community that is enveloped in courage, spontaneity, and aspirations for good work

Epilogue

We anticipate with great hope a new creation adorned by the songs of poets, imagination of artists, voices of prophets, hearts of healers, wisdom of mystics, fruits of creation, joy of children, and all those who listen with the ears of the soul and long for epiphanies at the edge of their unspoken hunger for sacredness and depth.

As we listen deeply to the invitation at this defining moment, we respond to the challenge to integrate our longing with the experience of sacredness and depth, an experience that will heal all separateness—the spirit and the street, vision and despair, ritual and rigidity, a wounded heart and a gorgeous planet—and create a new vision, soul eyes through which we perceive and celebrate a vision, a story of interconnectedness and common action.

As we ponder this defining moment and anticipate the future, we take up the challenge to be present where the future is in the process of being born, participating in its creation. Perhaps it is here that we will satisfy our longing and become a new people enveloped in a land of beauty, prompted by gestures of balance, harmony, and peace.

In sum, engaged cosmology explores the operative dynamics present in contemplative, liberation, and creation theologies and nurtures a resacralized world of harmony, balance, and peace through geo-justice (the translation of the principles of differentiation, communion, and interiority into cultural form), and the alignment of the powers of the cosmos with approaches to cultural transformation (personal, social, and ecological).

Component	Approach	Description
Longing of soul	Contemplation	Integrates your life through an awareness and awakening to your interior life to more deeply penetrate the mystery of the interdependence of all things
Longing of life	Liberation	Nurtures critical reflection on humanity's relationship to the world for the sake of transformation
Longing of Earth	Creation	Celebrates the new cosmic story, an awakened mysticism, and the awesome beauty of creating art, culminating in compassion and justice
Longing of the divine	Mystical and engaged cosmology	Promotes a dynamic relationship between contemplation, liberation, and creation that results in aligning the powers of the universe with the dynamics of cultural transformation

We look toward the future with gratitude for those on whose shoulders we stand. Our hearts are stirred and our souls awakened to the awe and wonder of the universe. A new consciousness permeates our souls. We feel inspired, alive. We act in new ways.

This new awareness also presents a challenge: how to translate our new consciousness into concrete strategies for change. To meet this challenge requires a commitment to preserve the integrity of the new cosmology and the consciousness that accompanies it. At the same time, we develop approaches to apply this new awareness to strategies for change.

Turning Toward Home

As we look to the future, in a sense, we turn toward home. As Thomas Berry would say, it's like "riding a horse and buggy" and turning toward home. When we feel the horse drawn toward its destination, a fresh energy empowers its journey, and we move at a more rapid and enthusiastic pace.

Such a turning toward will be a second Exodus: a time like that of the Copernican Revolution, when humanity was freed of the illusion that Earth was the center of the universe, and everything revolved around it. This second Exodus will require new myths and stories; a new master narrative; a new geography of soul, life, Earth, and the divine.

The days and moments ahead will require a Paschal mystery moment: a profound letting go and dying into the world before us and the worldview we have known.

The new life that will emerge among us will be marked by the birth of a new world order, a new meta-religious understanding, a new perception of the divine, a new politics and economics, and a new meaning of peace.

This transformation will be a rebirth that will call on and access both the creative and collective energy of the past, as well as the fresh visions and dreams being born in the hearts and minds of people today.

A new meaning of love will be nurtured in the embrace of all those relationships that hold us together in this new world, this new web of life.

As we turn toward home and reflect on our origins, new images will emerge: images of hope for a better tomorrow and images that respond to our longing for sacredness and depth.

As we stand here at the edge of our longing, positioned at the threshold of sacredness and depth, images of tomorrow emerge into consciousness bringing a new vision of hope to a world immersed in anxiety.

Hope from a new vision of monastery whose architecture is created out of the dynamic relationships that are nurtured by the wonder of the universe and our place in the future.

Hope from a fresh vision of novitiate, where each person's cosmological imagination reveals what it means to be human in an unfolding universe.

Hope from a renewed sense of home, an experience whereby we are reenergized to heal the wound of homelessness and become energized for the journey, like a horse who enthusiastically gallops when pointed toward home.

Hope from a gallery of beauty that touches every soul and reminds us of the gorgeous planet that invites us to commune and be at one.

Within this galaxy of images resides a unity, a healing oneness that unites point zero and ground zero, and all that is a manifestation of beauty to heal our longing for sacredness and depth.

At the close of one spring semester when I taught at the Sophia Center, the students planted a small oak tree in the Peace Garden on campus. We knew none of us would likely be there when that little sapling had become a tall oak. Yet, without the planting, watering, and care, there would be no tall oak. The work of engaged cosmology is to plant trees and to keep alive a hope-filled promise of a better tomorrow.

Each of us is like a tree of life, with our roots placed deeply in the earth, giving birth to a new economic system of sustainability and diversity: a trunk of biocracy and a fully functioning democracy; branches of a meta-religious movement, an Ecozoic council that supports, nurtures, and motivates all initiatives toward a more mutually enhancing relationship with Earth; and leaves that represent the wisdom of all genders and traditions, and a deepening commitment to a preferential option for Earth.

Another Name for Mystery

Where can I go to find
a place of comfort and rest,
where can I find a place
of listening and wisdom?
How can I find a place
where each passing day
awakens a fresh vision,
a place called tomorrow,
when tomorrow may never come?
Today I am without a home,
without origin or belonging,
yet I am born anew each day.
Today, yesterday, and tomorrow,
each another name for the cosmos,
for change, for the mystery of it all.

Foundation for Prolonged Engagement

This is and can be a "second Genesis," a threshold in time, a defining moment, a new beginning. It is time for a new Exodus as well: a moment to liberate our worldviews, cultural work, and spiritual practice from the confinement of conformity and outmoded approaches. A mystical and engaged cosmology embraces both the ancient and new, cultural and cosmic pathways to wisdom in order to heal our endangered planet and declining culture. An engaged cosmology will strive to make all things new, embrace the beauty of the present moment and the awe and wonder it brings to our lives.

As we move forward into an engaged cosmology through the dynamic interaction of vision/dream, engagement/action, and soul work/spiritual practice, we are mindful of the wisdom of the prophets of the past. Our acts of creativity and compassion cannot be confined to preordained methods or prescribed tactics. Rather, our approach is that every context is new, every challenge unique. The themes of engaged cosmology and the dynamics of dream, action, and soul work are designed to focus and energize our efforts. These approaches represent a converging wisdom of cultural work and cosmological consciousness. They are guidelines for a future yet to be born.

Three principles are necessary to insure a prolonged participation in engaged cosmology: vision/dream, engagement/action, and soul work/spiritual practice.

Vision/Dream

The vision/dream gains access to a profound urge that invites us to go further, to keep hope alive and cross the threshold into a better tomorrow. The vision/dream makes it possible to imagine how our world could be, to become receptive to those revelatory moments that alter and illuminate our lives. The vision/dream makes it possible for us to live in unprecedented ways. When we dream, we gain access to passion and compassion. We take our lives in our own hands and become deeply committed to do what needs to be done.

Engagement/Action

Through conscientious action, we create culture and build a bridge into the new era that awaits us. We become visually literate, see the world as it is, and are committed to create a world as we would like it to be. Our action is guided by the lessons learned from cosmology and cultural transformation.

With Dr. Martin Luther King, Jr., we are convinced that "the arc of the universe is long and bends toward justice." Our action becomes a celebration of the interdependence of all things, freedom for all sentient beings, and the primary revelation that is present everywhere in creation. Through conscious engagement, we become poet and politician, infused with a renewed ability to act. Through reciprocity and trust, we imagine and create a world where beauty can shine forth.

Soul Work/Spiritual Practice

Soul work challenges us to become transparent and fully present to life. We pay attention to existence and attune our lives to the unfolding dynamics of the universe. Through spiritual practice we gain courage and sustain our participation to create a better world: a world punctuated with dramatic moments of transformation and challenge that reveal and intensify the deep mystery that is operative in everyday existence, a world where we discover that our deepest longing comes from a cosmic and sacred source. Soul work is an expression of gratitude and a search for meaning.

Prolonged Engagement

Engaged cosmology integrates consciousness and conscience, thought and action. This integral awareness nurture a theory-and-practice approach. Our cosmological vision finds expression in collective action. Through awareness of the interdependence of all things (contemplation), the commitment to set all creatures free (liberation), and an intimate relationship with the natural world (creation), we set out to develop strategies for the important work that lies ahead.

In a world withering with the onslaught of terrorism, nuclear proliferation, military expansion, and poverty for the many and affluence for the few, a new wisdom and activism are urgently needed and longed for. The new synthesis of consciousness and action outlined in the contours of an engaged cosmology support the prolonged participation required to embrace cosmic consciousness and take action in the world to heal what is broken and renew the face of Earth.

The process of prolonged engagement is nurtured by a trinitarian approach that has its basis in the spectrum theology of contemplation (soul work), liberation (action), and creation (dream), energized by the dynamics of the universe (interiority, differentiation, and communion) and by the spirituality that flows from the experience of mystery, creativity, and compassion.

Principles for prolonged engagement	Component of spectrum theology	Principles of the universe	Spiritual experience
Soul work/ Spiritual practice	Contemplation	Interiority	Mystery
Engagement/action	Liberation	Differentiation	Creativity
Vision/dream	Creation	Communion	Compassion

New Venture

We venture forth today
to go beyond our longing,
to reinvent the future,
to integrate science and art,
to become both a poet and a politician,
to focus on the quest for the true self,
to allow surprise to upset our plans,
to become immersed in holy mystery.

Developing a Practice

The practice of an engaged cosmology is developed within the context of a base community. Participants gather to pose questions, explore their deepest longing, and listen attentively to one another. As they examine their responses in light of their spiritualities of contemplation, liberation, and creation, they are moved into action.

The questions to be discussed include the following.

Longing of Soul

What thresholds of sacredness and depth have been most helpful in your process (e.g., listening, remembering, letting go, heeding the prophets, practicing compassion, relating to the little ones, honoring creation, envisioning)?

How has your reflection on these themes expanded your capacity to penetrate the mystery of existence?

What actions will enhance your ability to respond to the longing of soul and contribute to the awakening of your interior life?

Longing of Life

What encounters with a person or group (e.g., illness of self or a loved one, people of justice, poverty, war, or political conflict) have opened your life to a deeper embrace of the mystery and meaning of life?

How have these moments of intimate connection with others transformed the nature of your relationships and reconstituted your perception of the world?

What action are you prompted to engage in to heal, strengthen, and transform your relationships with others in the world?

Longing of Earth

What experiences with creation do you recall that shaped and influenced your life?

Have you participated in a group focused on ecology or environmentalism?

How has your experience of the natural world awakened in you a sense of sacredness, appreciation of beauty, and feelings of compassion?

How will you respond to the ecological devastation of our time?

What actions will you take to resacralize Earth?

Longing of the Divine

How can we become empowered to respond to the needs of this moment within the context of an emergent universe, with attention to the revelatory awareness of the interior life, the human struggle for authentic freedom, and a growing consciousness that all our experiences are connected and sacred?

How has your world view and religious tradition prepared you to be critical of and responsive to this particular moment of grace?

What actions does a mystical and engaged cosmology prompt you to undertake to bring peace, joy, and compassion to our world?

About the Author

Jim Conlon was born in Canada in 1936. He received a degree in chemistry from Assumption University of Windsor, and later in theology from the University of Western Ontario, and a PhD from Union Institute and University. Deeply moved by the impact of the second Vatican Council, the civil rights movement, and the Vietnam War, Jim moved from pastoral work to the streets. He was the recipient of the 2013 Thomas Berry Award.

For more information and a complete list of Jim's published works, see: www.jimconlon.net.

Contact: Springbank: 843-372-6311 or
         springbank@springbankretreat.org

Milton Keynes UK
Ingram Content Group UK Ltd.
UKHW021532050124
435394UK00009B/42

9 798986 410067